EMBRACING LIFE

By the author

EMBRACING LIFE

CELEBRATE YOUR SELF

YOUR CHILD'S SELF-ESTEEM

Dorothy Corkille Briggs

EMBRACING LIFE

Growing Through Love and Loss

DOUBLEDAY & COMPANY, INC.
GARDEN CITY, NEW YORK
1985

For details on any material marked with an asterisk,
please consult the notes on pages 127–28.

Library of Congress Cataloging in Publication Data
Briggs, Dorothy Corkille
Embracing Life.
1. Conduct of life.   2. Meaning (Psychology)
3. Love.   4. Separation (Psychology)   I. Title.
BF637.C5B75   1985   158'.1
ISBN: 0-385-23000-1
Library of Congress Catalog Card Number: 84-25946

DEDICATION

In a very real sense this book is an expression of gratitude to all of you whose lives have touched mine: family, friends, teachers, students, clients. You may be sure you have each had an important impact on my life.

I appreciate:

· June Schwarzmann's skill in editing, especially the sequential flow of ideas. This is a special gift to me from a lady of love and caring.

· Ann Cullen for typing parts of the manuscript under tight time deadlines.

· Billy Burg, aged ten, whose life is a walking testimonial to this book's theme.

· Karen Van Westering, my editor at Doubleday, who has been a crucial part of bringing this message to you.

I thank each of you for being in my life.

DOROTHY CORKILLE BRIGGS
Rancho Palos Verdes
California

CONTENTS

Some day,
    after mastering the winds, the waves,
                the tides, and gravity,
we will harness for God the energies of love.
            And then, for the second time
        in the history of the world,
    man will have discovered fire.
                    PIERRE TEILHARD DE CHARDIN

EMBRACING LIFE

OUTREACH

D o you remember the story of Jonathan Livingston Seagull? He learned to dive beyond limitation. And then he wanted to reach out to share what he'd learned. He wanted others to experience the Way. To transcend old limitations. To move beyond the old conditioning. To maximize what is possible. He wanted to share the taste of new wine. Transformation.

This offering is shared with the hope that it may clarify your purpose and meaning. We are each here to make a difference. And I believe that means we use love, loss, life to empower us to more fully give our gift to the world. And in so doing, our own lives become sweeter . . . no matter what.

With change one of the few constants these days, this book focuses on how to use change victoriously. It is about overcoming—indeed embracing—whatever. And that requires finding your unique song. Once you find your Heart-song—your purpose—nothing and no one can keep you from singing it clearly.

You are an unrepeatable miracle. A first in the universe. None carbon-copy you. As an incredible gift, you touch many lives. You count. You and I are each asked to let our song be heard . . . be it a simple resonance or an aria of grandeur. The size of it doesn't matter. Your *particular* song does.

Many nugget ideas have fused for me over the years through each person whose life has touched mine, by each happening, by how I've experienced my journey.

With this writing I offer them to you. They are thoughts to mull over. Those you resist most strongly you might want to put on the back burner of your mind for simmering now and tasting later.

I invite you to dive beyond old conditioning, old beliefs. To release old limitations of what you believe possible. Perhaps these thought-gifts will trigger that release.

The healing power of the human mind is dawning. An incredible explosion of what can be is surfacing. That we can make our lives victorious, no matter what, is to become empowered . . . to finally come into our own.

When you catch the vision, you begin to see the Way. To see what is possible means to become aware . . . to awake. It means using that awareness, that awakened state, to reframe relationships, loss, life. It means rejoining body, mind and spirit to become fully whole.

For when all is said and done, each of us *is* a Light. Each of us is being invited by Life to come Home and then go forth as a Lamplighter. Our world needs your Heart Light.

May you let your light so shine . . .

RELATIONSHIPS

Relationships! Networks to childhood family. To mate and children. To friends, co-workers, neighbors, all those you connect with. Relationship . . . that vibrational stuff that goes on between people. That invisible web line that carries the transactions.

Relationships could be so easy. The issues seem simple enough. How often they are not. What is it we want from them? Where does the snafu lie?

We each need to love and be loved. We need to feel valued and treated with respect. We want to be spared judgment and put-downs. We'd like to iron out conflicts to mutual satisfaction. We want to enjoy and bridge over in meaningful ways. Consciously we want this. Not a tall order.

The sticky wicket begins with our very uniqueness. Each is a "first" trying to connect with other "firsts." This automatically means built-in difference.

Yet, paradoxically, our needs are alike. How does a piccolo connect with a snare drum? A violin with a tuba? A challenge for every composer. The same challenge for every human being. How do two total "differences" connect to create harmony, not discord?

This very struggle consumes so much of our energy, over

and over. Our world and how we experience it seems so clear. Why can't others understand? And agree!

As if uniqueness were not challenge enough, there is a far larger hurdle. Invisible, yet powerful, the issue of self-esteem directly affects all our relationships.

If self-worth is shaky, I am a self-doubter. My hidden agenda, often unknown to me, is to gather proof of my OK-ness. *I need to orchestrate relationships and life to get such proof.*

If self-doubt is intense, I may need to play Top Dog and call *all* the shots. I freeze on having to direct, manage, faultfind and win. *I can cooperate only on my terms.* Flexibility and mutuality are not options for me.

If self-doubt is mild, I may need to prove my importance not so much to others as to myself. My hunger is more to gather approval. I am not into "shaping others and life up." Rather *I am pushed to caretake, please and overgive.* Even at the risk of personal integrity. Unwittingly I may permit others to take advantage or even "victimize" me.

If self-esteem is low, I am a self-hater. Then my need is to gather proof of my Not-OKness. *Unconsciously, I set myself up to lose.* My energy goes into self-sabotage. I arrange my life and relationships accordingly. I place impossible demands on my-self and all others. I freeze on impossible expectations and forever focus on what is wrong. I figure out how to undo all good coming my way—be it relational, vocational, financial.

When self-esteem is low or shaky, difference in close others is a threat. Relating has little to do with what is right or needed. Rather it has to do with who is right, who'll win, who gets done in.

If self-esteem is high, I don't have hidden agenda items. My self-confidence frees my energy for constructive giving of my talents to others and the world. I refuse to sacrifice integrity by placating at all costs. But I am fluid enough to cooperate. I see positives and can afford to see others' point of view as well as my own. Developing my competencies flows naturally. I am not driven.

I don't play perfectionist, for I accept my strengths and my foibles nondefensively. I can afford to admit to myself and others when I fall short. I can risk standing up for my beliefs. My self-affirmation allows me to affirm others. I have nothing to prove or destroy. I'm not into *who;* rather I am into *what* is right. I focus on how we can work together.

Self-confidence frees me to enjoy and facilitate others' triumphs as well as my own. Solid self-worth gives me a base that makes jealousy, threat, possessiveness and hostility places where I choose not to dwell. My very self-confidence lessens such needs.

So relationships are a great challenge by their very nature: *uniqueness and the degree of self-worth come into play in every transaction we have with all others.*

Yet a third, less prevalent, factor can operate to create distress in relationships: physiological imbalances. Chemical and neurological imbalances in the brain and nervous system; the misfiring of brain cells; allergic reactions; hormonal imbalances and tissue damage, all impact to create behaviors that dramatically affect relationships and how one lives life. Such factors need to be checked before assuming that relational snafus are purely psychological.

Barring physical problems, most relationship stresses come from the fact that we connect with others from the personality level—the Conditioned Self.

Because we are single individuals, most of us think we are single Selves. Quite the contrary. Each of us is literally a family of subselves:

- **the Real Self.** This is the essential or spiritual You— the You that is totally unique and unlike any other.

- **the Rational Self.** This is the part that is in contact with reality, that estimates probabilities, that problem-solves.

- **the Observer Self.** It is aware of how the other sub-selves are operating. (In many this Self is too often fast asleep. But it can be awakened.)

- **the Critic.** This part acts as judge, punisher, and looks for what is wrong. It has unrealistically high expectations and is convinced it has all the answers. It's into calling the shots.

- **the Nurturer.** This subself is like a kindly grandparent: firm, yet supportive. It is "for" you. It gives unconditional love. Yet it is not overindulgent. It is empathic, keeps expectations reasonable and sees what is right.

- **the Playful Child.** This Self is free and open, creative and expressive. It is intuitive and impulsive. It may need limiting at times. In many adults this subself is almost a closet skeleton—simply denied. In some it runs wild.

- **the Not-OK Self.** This subself is rebellious or overcompliant. It believes it is unlovable or that it is loveworthy only on condition that it live up to the Critic's standards. It feels guilty, bad and inadequate.

The Real Self and the Playful Child come with our birth. The Real Self is of God; it is pure Love. There are the rare Gandhis, Mother Teresas and Schweitzers who daily relate from this soul level.

The rest of the listed subselves are often lumped together and called the Conditioned Self—as if it were one, rather than many selves. These selves come into being as a result of the conditions around us as we grow.

Most of us mortals do not relate from the soul level daily. Rather we connect from the Conditioned Self. We relate over old, unmet childhood needs and defenses. Our core belief that we are unlovable and our need to feel important cause us to relate negatively if our childhoods were filled with deficit. Then we tend to "use" relationships to deny, pretend, prove or win. Therein lies the rub. Those hidden agendas mean we may come into relationships with an ax to grind. Or that others have one as they connect with us.

The Conditioned Self—coming from childhood—has holes, deficits, expectations, needs, and scared places that it tries to work out in today's relationships. And old wounds get triggered off by situations today. Often the neediness in one plays off the neediness in the other. And then varying degrees of stress and pain result.

The challenge is to be *aware* of our own and others' conditioned scripts. And grow free of them.

When a relationship presents problems, far too many these days believe they have only to change the name, the face and the place. And serenity will surely follow. They forget they take all their subselves and unfinished business into every relationship. So, increasingly, we have serial relationships that only replay the same scene—with variations.

Others stay with the same relationship but one wants to change the original contract on which the coupleship was formed. Yet the partner may not go for that idea.

A typical example is the couple with the unwritten contract "Let's you and me take care of me." All goes well until Caretaker tires and wants a new deal. Responsible tires of pulling the weight. But Irresponsible doesn't want to take up the oar.

The grownup "Child" may want to stand on his or her

own feet. But the "Parent" would be out of the job that brings proof of being needed. "Parent" wants the "Child" to grow up but may sabotage each effort. The unconscious saboteurs—defenses born in childhood—want to stay with the status quo. They have old scores to settle, old survival strategies to cling to.

The unconscious bargain that cemented the original coupling gets into deadlock—impasse. Solution?

Avoid focus on the *people* involved. Instead scrutinize and renegotiate the contract—the script being acted out. Look for patterns that simply rehash the hash over and over. To do this means attending to our *own* Conditioned Self. And finding legitimate ways to get its needs met, rather than using today's relationship as the stage for working out old childhood needs. Bait-dangling and bait-taking—old survival strategies—are far too rampant. The pity is most of it is not conscious.

Each coupling—whether it's lovers, mates, friends—ordinarily has its honeymoon period. Disillusionment follows as familiarity breaks the illusions.

Next comes the power struggle . . . most often straight from early childhood decisions on how to survive in the world. Loner picks Social (just like his or her sister) and later feels inferior because the other shines. Charger picks Hang Loose (just like his or her father) and subsequently tries to get the other to take hold. Each may play "if it weren't for you." Each unknowingly struggles to settle old childhood business.

Impasses are broken when both own their part in the stress and work on their personal unfinished business. This can only occur with total self-honesty. And a willingness to change, practice new behavior and wriggle free of conditioning that created the "hang-up" in the first place.

Often relationships break up at the power-struggle stage.

When a couple lack common values, ethics and goals, there is no glue to hold them together once the games are thrown out.

Changing the lifelong patterns of the Conditioned Self is not easy. But it *is* possible, especially when pain is strong. That very pain is friend. It motivates us to try new behavior. If negative scripts are not changed, they tend to worsen with age. So when relationships stress, we are given an invitation to learn the lesson. And get free of old, outmoded patterns that imprison.

The sharings that follow are spot ideas to trigger your thinking and study. Hopefully they will spur you to see your script more clearly. And to gather the willingness to chip away outmoded constraints.

As you grow more whole, your present relationships can become more whole. But it takes two to renegotiate and requires good faith.

Sadly, sometimes only one is willing to change. The other remains glued to the Conditioned Self. They want more of the same rather than growth. Then they can continue to act out the same tired script. And reap the same tired pain. Some have a commitment to stress and self-destructiveness. Make sure that is not your script.

Whatever you do to you, you will tend to do to others. All relationships are colored by one's relationship to Self. All each of us can do is get our own act together. And to realize that some are dedicated to nonchange in themselves. Sad but true.

Each of us is, however, only accountable for how we walk in life. How others walk is their answer to God. We are not responsible for their walk. We are only responsible for our own.

May your walk be in compassion and understanding. If you falter in that understanding, work on it. One day it will come.

It can be done!

You and I can reframe life's experiences and move into light. Gwenet's sharing poignantly bears this out:

> I feel so many emotions. My mind spins. I can't be sure of the direction for my life. I want to be a fire of enthusiasm, not just a tiny candle flame.
>
> I've learned much about myself. But I'm impatient to know so much more. I panic that my perfectionism will keep my wheels forever spinning . . . striving . . . more, more.
>
> I am angry at the world for crushing my sense of importance and personal worth. I feel forced to strive to be secure with *myself* and find peace.
>
> I want to shrink all the painful memories, erase the emotions and see the events without feeling. I want the past to be just historical facts. Not these unwept tears crying out to be free!
>
> I want the heavy load of feeling needy, lost and hating the inside person to go away. I want all that inner stuff collected up and filed away in a mental box. I want to scrub my mind clean of every grimy picture etched there by a child's anguished heart.
>
> I want to see those child-made vivid scenes as homework left there by that child. Left to record her being, her reality, her need for some historical evidence of her presence in the world. No matter what the scenes, *they prove* that the child *did* exist. Even though others failed to acknowledge that. Failed to acknowledge her physical presence in the world and her *specialness.*
>
> Why those etchings still? Why do they still adorn the walls of the adult mind? Why hasn't the artist-now-

grown replaced those childish scribblings with my adult mastery of today?

These early paintings are etched so deeply. They were not made to be wiped away unceremoniously. Not made to be cast aside for something better. They were the best that that oh-so-wee little person could do at the time. They were not made to be lost forever, leaving a nothingness, a total absence of her even *being* in those early days.

Then why do I still feel pain? Why am I stuck fast? Why are they not worn away by the constant dusting they've had? With each return to that almost sacred secret spot, the clearing of dust reveals old pains still stuck . . . stuck after all these years.

Maybe the pain is to remind the little child to go back. To remember the little child who wept her childhood tears. *Maybe the pain is to teach me to love her and make things all right. To hold her in my wise adult arms and to soothe her aching heart and searching soul.*

Who else knows her so well, so deeply? I am the one who has *always* been with her, sharing the feelings of hope that someday there will be a time for understanding. Who else but the grownup me can bring her that wisdom she's so long thirsted for? Who else can quiet her questions over the past? Who else can lift her tender yearning soul and make her *feel* her specialness?

Thank you, Lord. Peace . . . at last!

GWENET PORTER

Intimacy

Have you ever thought, "This Other is not who I thought she or he was"? And you feel disillusion.

The Other *is* who the Other *is*.

Ask gently, "Who created the illusion?" So often the eye of the beholder.

————◦◦◦————

Why is it we so fiercely resist giving up our illusions? About Others? Ourselves? Life?

Often we choose not to see what *is* because *to see would force an action or decision we don't want to take.* Maybe facing Real hurts too much. But each time we deny reality, we eventually pay the price. Real can hurt. But Real can be trusted.

————◦◦◦————

I cannot be close and affirm another until I dare to be close and affirm myself. "I" comes before "we." I bring me into each relationship. It is my job to make me strong in Love so I bring you a whole person. Otherwise, I cannot adequately love you.

Your self-affirmation energizes you so that you are free to love me. Your self-wipeout lessens your ability to love me. Whole relationships ask each of us to bring in relatively whole people.

————◦◦◦————

"My way of seeing it is the *only* way of seeing it" is closed, no-win monologue.

————◦◦◦————

If we persist in denying reality, we get skinned knees or end up with a bucketful of unfilled dreams.

———⋘⋙———

Rage comes from feeling powerless.

———⋘⋙———

In so many relationships, the undercurrent-yet-silent request is "Give me what Papa or Mama would not give me."

———⋘⋙———

You can be loyal to a person from your past *without being loyal to their way of being in the world.*

———⋘⋙———

How dare you! Who gave you permission to upset me so?
I did.
Oh!

———⋘⋙———

The human being needs intimacy to find meaning, to thrive. But many, having been hurt in childhood, now go for counterfeit relationships. These couplings hold intimacy's *form* but not its *substance.*

Those fearful of genuine intimacy may use power over others to keep them close. They are controllers. Others may "agree" to be "victims" to keep the Persecutor connected. Some reel in others with guilt-producing tactics so that obligation glues the person in place.

All such connectings doom intimacy. Such unconscious manipulations prevent the real "I-Thou" connection. Which is what intimacy is all about. Caring, shar-

ing, hearing with heart, as coequals, spells intimacy and
love.

———❧———

Some can take closeness only briefly. Then they
"must" pull back. This action is a statement about their
Inner Child's needs and not necessarily one about your
person.

Watch taking such pullbacks personally if that is
their pattern.

———❧———

If you do not let others know what you prefer or
dislike, you ask them to play crystal ball gazer. Few are
adept at this game.

Let it be known.

———❧———

Giving you a computer printout of my day, my
thoughts, gives us "head intimacy." Cold. Doesn't do
the trick.

Sharing my feelings, my experiential world, lets you
into my heart.

If you discount my feelings, rational or not, intimacy
is wiped out. *Only relationships that honor feelings build close-*
ness and love.

———❧———

Opposites attract but compatibles find more bridges
for connecting. And tend to walk to a similar drummer.

———❧———

The Constitution guarantees freedom of speech. But
so many have unknowingly given up that right. They

are locked into the speech of the Conditioned Self. They can only speak as Complainer, Victim, Pleaser, Denier, Loner, Rescuer, Controller, Noncommitter and so on and on and on.

Have you given up your right to *free* speech in your relationships? Are you locked into one or two party lines? Do you give any of the above subselves star billing? And pay the price?

With awareness and effort you can rewrite your script. Then game-free intimacy is born.

———⦾———

Some can commit; some go for flit.

Flitters fear intimacy. They are forever in a double bind—wanting closeness yet fearful of it. Such folks set themselves up for loss every time. Their fear makes them push others away.

Committers heard one language in childhood; flitters, another. Do not assume because you both speak English that you speak the same tongue where intimacy is concerned.

If intimacy is what you want, seek those who speak your same "language."

———⦾———

Some folks are relational. They want to connect to people. Others are nonrelational. They prefer interacting with ideas, things. Strange how these two attract. And then each pushes the game of Match Me.

The great energy drain!

———⦾———

The basis of the Inner Child's neediness is hunger for approval—fear of rejection. As a child, you truly *did* need outer approval. It was your lifeline. But as an adult, *you* need to "feed" your own Child Within.

When you nurture this Inner Child, then you *enjoy* and *prefer* others' approval. But you won't pretzel or con to get it. Nor allow others to involve you in such games.

This shift from *needing* outer approval to inner self-confidence means you do not come to relationships from hunger. Rather, you come from fullness. Not from desert. But for dessert.

———◦◦———

Would you let a small child grab you by the nose and say, "I'm going to run your life"? Ridiculous! Yet many adults are totally controlled by their Inner Child's old survival strategies.

The Inner Child creates bodyguards to ensure safety in the world. Some common bodyguards are:

- pretzeling to get approval
- not getting close
- staying in charge
- coattailing another's strengths
- making nice for others, never for self
- floundering to get attention
- walling off
- acting tough
- pretending "it" doesn't exist
- being perfect

These are *Self preservers.* They once had payoff and made sense earlier. They were appropriate for that particular environment of long ago and considering the child's limited resources at the time. And its immaturity.

But the lifesaver of childhood becomes the noose of adulthood unless maladaptive strategies are tossed out.

The price tag in adulthood for no longer appropriate bodyguards: useless burning of energy, staying chained to the past, and unending manipulations. *Mature intimacy cannot be achieved with them.*

Yet the Inner Child of today's adult believes letting go of bodyguards—those old "lifesavers"—means *emotional suicide.* To let go of them is to trust the void. It *is* scary.

The largest destroyer of intimacy is *fear of closeness.* Childhood outreach brought negatives. It was futile; the Other did not connect. Or you got clobbered, controlled or engulfed, abandoned. Survival? Pull in, build walls, pretend. But do not get close.

Solution? Reassure your Inner Child that you are older, wiser, and have many more resources than it did long ago. Let it know you are its future . . . its Nurturer and Protector . . . benign and providing. Let it know it can turn to *you* for what it needs. Decide to nurture it today and daily. Supportive self-talk is vital.

Childhood shoes pinch and misshape adult feet.

Get new shoes to walk in.

Self-responsibility

Trees are smarter than people. Flat out! They do not resist outer reality; they adjust. Arid clime? They create leaves that reduce water loss. Slanted gorge? Trunks curve to upright. Frigid weather? Leaves drop; juices retreat till conditions change. Trees self-preserve appropriately—survive—cope creatively.

We people throw up pain conductors: *shoulds.* "Others 'should' be different." "Why 'should' it happen to me?" We resist the unwanted with all the power at our command. *Trees would be long gone if they ran life as people do.*

Survival requires working with our "local" reality. The outer is circumstance. The inner holds solution. Yes, we have much to learn from trees. They teach one of life's great lessons: wholeness requires that we deal with reality. And we are each responsible for *how* we deal with it.

We can buck it or back it.

"Self-love, my liege, is not so vile a sin as Self-neglecting."

SHAKESPEARE

If I refuse to become whole in my own right, I ask to be excused from natural laws. Nature will not be commanded. It asks all living things to unfold as designed. Needful dependency brakes growth.

Relentlessly, nature nudges for flower. Blossom is the purpose. We grow ourselves. Or abort our own bloom. Interdependency? Yes. Dependency for adults? No. Not for fully functioning human beings.

When we do what is right for our own integrity, we do what is right for the integrity of those around us.

The need for approval can tempt us to sell our integrity. Such a sale is needless because it does not work. Not with peer or child. Trying to make it with the Other at all costs only encourages the Other to exploit. We lose the Other's respect and our own.

Your integrity is what you face life with. Never put it up for sale.

The Other may expect you to salute, give endlessly, take repeatedly, not be impacted. But it is you who agree to that contract. Do you really want to?

Fair was never promised.

Fear of losing a relationship, peer or child, means we are up for grabs. It leaves us wide open to manipulation . . . imprisoned by that fear. Eventually, we can become immobilized.

I am free to make all kinds of choices. But I, and all around me, will pay the consequences of those choices. No one is an island. Every choice of mine impacts me *and* others. I am responsible for my choices and their impact on others. Situational ethics and do-your-own-thing hoopla notwithstanding.

We only fool ourselves if we set aside self-honesty. What button do we poke that pushes the stress? How would we feel on the receiving end of what we dish out?

Guilty answers don't solve problems. Changed attitudes and behaviors do.

———————◅∽▻———————

Values are guideposts that blueprint growth. Our values show by how we walk life—with ourselves—with others. Values undergirded by Love empower both giver and receiver.

———————◅∽▻———————

Friendship is a limited safety zone. Some zones are far larger than others. But each has a time and a place called "unavailable."

The more friends you have, the less you expect any one person to be all things. The broader your safety base, the fewer disappointments, the less the pain.

———————◅∽▻———————

Putting your happiness and well-being *totally* in another's hands keeps you forever dependent. And vulnerable. The other dies, leaves? You bleed, dangle.

———————◅∽▻———————

Enjoy the Other's strengths; protect your Self against the Other's weaknesses.

———————◅∽▻———————

To be continually on the Other's case is to avoid taking care of my own. It is *not* my job to grow you.

———————◅∽▻———————

Who I become, how I unfold, what I do with my gifts is strictly up to me. It *is* my job to grow me.

Others cannot do it *to* me. Or *for* me.

Responsibility collectors get to do just that. They tend to sponge it up with children, friends, mates. And they get to have burnout.

A vast difference exists when you are *responsible for* yourself and *to* others (not *for* others). Then you avoid burnout.

And others get to do their own homework.

Avoid making something out of nothing—a waste. Or nothing out of something—a waste.

We all speak the language we hear spoken. Just so, in today's relationships, we may be mimicking parental scripts.

If your parent was a "woman user," you may unconsciously follow suit. If your parent lived that "men are no good," your attitude may match. If you experienced parents in loving relationship with each other, you likely repeat the pattern.

If your relationships are stressed, look to see if you could be following an old script. Are you talking the "psychological language" you heard spoken? Lack of awareness is the same as no choice. Become aware.

With awareness and conscious decision you can change the script. You *can* shift from old compulsion to new choice.

Anger is a second feeling. First comes pain, shock, helpless, whatever. Anger is the "fight back." It is energy directed against facing that first hurt.

When we deny that *first* feeling, it can remain converted as anger to insist we take up the sword. If we don't deal with original pain directly, it deals with us. Eventually, it controls our lives.

We may spend the rest of our time here electing various people to hang that anger on. And then wonder why we are unhappy.

Someone "did you in"? There's a lesson there. Find it and then the lesson will not need to be repeated. Become aware of what *you* may or may not have done that contributed to the situation. Then you can avoid that pitfall, if you choose.

Each happening in life is to teach us what we have yet to learn. Bless your mistakes. Hopefully, each one teaches one.

As You Believe

Two caterpillars watched a butterfly. One said to the other, "You'll never get me up in one of those things!"

Adults who refuse to grow up (an unconscious choice not to change) turn their relationships into symbiosis. They refuse to use their own resources. They expect others to fill their gaps. They do not believe in their own potential to fly.

When you honestly look at what you do in your relationships, are you refusing to grow?

———◦◦◦———

I do this for you and expect the same in return. (This expectation may not even be conscious.) Then I run up the flag of "unfair" if you fail to come through. Golden Rule contracts make life a joy. But the name on that contract may be only your own. It is often only your *assumption* that the Other's name is on the line. Check out your assumptions on this point to avoid disappointment in relationships.

———◦◦◦———

The Inner Child unconsciously tries to re-create the past in today's relationships. Even if painful.

Irrational? No.

If you'd lived from birth through late teens in the Arctic and then moved to Arizona, you might well freeze your water bed, install frigid air conditioners and maybe import whale blubber. You'd want the familiar.

This is precisely what the Inner Child goes for—the known. *If the past held pain, the Inner Child seeks, indeed sabotages, today's good to get it.*

Patrick Henry said that the price of liberty is eternal vigilance. This truth holds for us personally. The *price of psychological liberty is eternal vigilance over the Inner Saboteur.* Otherwise, we recycle the childhood scenario of pain in relationship after relationship.

Unfinished childhood business needs to be worked through with a safe person, in a safe place. The formula is: Get the old, festered material out, release, forgive. Then visualize (see, hear, feel) the new positive relationship. Vivid mind pictures of the positive new situations or traits have proven power, as Olympic athletes have demonstrated. This "new" will become habit.

Inwardly *claim* positive beliefs about the Self. And guess what? Sunshine starts feeling better than Arctic blasts.

Expecting others to make me happy is my Inner Child's claim. It guarantees disappointment, vulnerability and dependency. Not what grownups need.

"I need predictability and the Other is unpredictable!" If 'tis so, isn't the unpredictability predictable? Function from that base.

None of us has the power to help another if that Other does not want help. It is only when the Other *allows us to touch* his or her life that *sometimes* we can midwife growth.

When pain crops up, look to an unmet expectation, a hope or belief you just tripped over. Look to a refusal on your part to take a new tack, a new stance or attitude. Are you holding on to a belief that needs changing given these conditions?

The negatively Conditioned Self ("the Not-OK Self") plays nonstop tapes in your head if you let it. Elect your own Nielsen rating committee. Cancel those overused reruns today. They were produced years ago in childhood by those whose hang-ups prevented their validating you.

Enough already!

―――――◦∽◦――――

Dr. Paul Brenner has pointed out that if you don't finish your unfinished childhood business, your future becomes your past.

―――――◦∽◦――――

Do you expect the loved Other to give what you won't give to yourself?

"Fill my bucket," "Meet my blueprints as I designed them," leave little room for uniqueness. Neediness can be a bottomless pit.

―――――◦∽◦――――

Takers gravitate to Givers. But Givers sign the line.

―――――◦∽◦――――

"Let me rescue you so I can feel important" often pairs with "Save me so I can resist your efforts." No-win situation for either. A dependency contract that becomes a pain trap.

―――――◦∽◦――――

A famous Scottish general, battle-weary and outnumbered by invading British, agonized through the night. Should he send his remaining men to certain death in the morning? Or should he save their lives and let Britain take Scotland?

No decision formed. As day broke, his eye fell on a tiny spider attempting to throw its first line to a twig. Repeatedly the spider threw the line and fell short. But it would not give up. It stayed with its purpose and doggedly repeated its mission. At long last the spider crossed the gap.

The general had his answer. He woke his troops, shared what he'd seen and said, "If a spider can do it, so can we."

That day his men descended to battle. Worn and badly outnumbered? Yes. But they were convinced, like the spider, they could win.

Today Scots have their own identity.

What of you?

Would you let a spider outpurpose you? Are you convinced that, no matter what, you can do it? Recall: it is done unto you as you believe.

Parenting

" 'You must be free to take a path whose end I have no need to know' is a helpful parental stance once children are grown."

MARGARET MEAD

———————⚬———————

Son? Daughter?

We are scheduled by nature to separate out from our family of origin. Theoretically, we become our own persons and then reconnect with parents, adult to adult.

Theory aside, some find they slip back to Child around parents and then fault them. But it is we who slip into Child.

Some cling to the old Child role. Some pendulum to opposite. Some are unfortunately asked as children to assume the role of caretaker adult. If you have older parents, you may find yourself in role reversal. Parents are now like children dependent on you.

It is the exception, not the rule, that the parent-child connection proceeds smoothly at each stage. As a present-day adult, it is important to name the reality of that special role, face the snafus and work creatively with them. Easier when self-esteem is high. But rarely accomplished without work. Yet the lessons to be learned go a long way toward making us compassionate and mature.

———— ⌒ ————

Overindulgence, martyrdom and overcontrol are not parenting. They are statements of our own personal needs.

———— ⌒ ————

"No" is at times the greatest gift of love I can give to my child. Ultimately my "no" allows that child to say "no" to itself. It's called tough love.

———— ⌒ ————

"Others often cannot get their hands on the issue until I get mine off." Letting go *appropriately* is part of loving our children.

JANIS OLSEN

———— ⌒ ————

Often it is not the child who is in pain, it is the parent. When, as a parent, I try to protect my child from natural consequences of its behavior, I literally cripple. I stymie growth.

———— ⌒ ————

"My mother loved me with all of her heart but not all of her time."

PEARL BUCK

———————⟨∾⟩———————

As a parent, I more fully nurture when my stance is: I don't know *how* your path will go. But I know *that* you'll make it. And that your trip will *differ* from mine.

Our faith in our youngsters becomes their faith in themselves.

Loving

Love is a way of being that allows those on the other end of us to come home to Center. Love sees the miracle of the Other. Love says "no" when we mean "no"; "yes," if appropriate. Love says, "I'm sorry," means it and corrects the behavior.

Love involves a willingness to deal with issues. It does not use the Other as a need-filler only. Love is not overprotecting. It allows the Other the dignity of his or her own pain. It does not seek to possess or demand the Other be clone. Love anchors in trust. Love releases the Other to be self-responsible. It does not pretend clay feet do not exist. Nor does it expect perfection.

Love is blind?

"In love" is.

Love is not.

It is wise to know the difference.

———————⟨∾⟩———————

We often forget that love is the only thing that is not lessened by giving it away. The deeper our caring, the deeper the love when we give it away.

———❧———

Love cannot be seen, touched or clutched. It can only be felt when it flows from an open heart.

———❧———

Do something nice for someone you love . . . don't try to change them. We are not in adult relationships to shape the Other up or to be shaped up . . . tempting as such is.

———❧———

Love is *not managing*. Neither is it the *refusal to be involved*. The fine line between is the challenge.

———❧———

We all need Love. But sometimes we substitute Bigger, More. These, however, leave a gnawing within— insatiable.

Love comes in tiny dailiness. In thoughtful concern, in outreach, in small moments of caring without strings —being there for the Other in spite of. It comes in a kind word, a soft glance, a phone call, a note, a slow pace, a gentle touch, an empathic heart.

Give these out freely and your cup overfloweth. Withhold and you never know Love. Now, today, those around you need you as a Love-er.

———❧———

Words of love are empty unless you feel the Other hears with heart. Empathy is a powerful *act* of love.

Words of love are empty if they are unmatched by behavior reflecting the Golden Rule.

Words of love are hollow without commitment and trust that glue the relationship even in times of storm.

Love is not a fair-weather commodity.

All the pills, all the booze, all the sex, all the money, all the fame, never bring Love.

The only thing that brings Love is giving it away. No substitutes work.

So often "I love you" means "I need you." Needing is not loving. It only charades as love. Songs, movies, novels, romantic notions notwithstanding.

Pluses and minuses are a package deal. We cannot have one without the other. Yet how many search for Mr., Ms. Right . . . expect only sunshine. They forget that sun without rain creates desert.

Another offers you love (friendship) as *they* spell out love (friendship). You might rather have it as *you* define love (friendship).

Lesson: Accept that their way of giving *is* their way of giving . . . quite different from yours. Otherwise, you can make a career of disappointment.

Our culture worships youth, sex and the perfect 10 body. How much more appropriate if we worshipped Love.

Love comes from giving, not demanding. Love is openhanded. It does not grasp. Love is valuing, cherishing without condition. When you truly stand in the Love Space, you cannot intentionally hurt another. Nor use the Other for your purposes. For Love is not using.

When we touch another with Love, we allow God to use us as channel.

Do I touch others with full focus, empathy, openness, realness, caring, walking the extra mile? Can I be trusted?

My answer yardsticks how *well* I love.

Contrary to popular belief, power comes not from getting but from giving. The only real power, the only real winning is the joy of committed Love.

Self-doubt, self-hate spawn destructiveness. Self-affirmation is the bedrock that prevents destructive behavior. We can only love others to the degree we affirm ourselves.

Are you a kindly grandparent to you—in your private self-talk? If not, why not?

If your Inner Shriveler is given star billing, you disempower your Self. It is imperative, if we would improve relationships, to learn the language of Love. And speak it to ourselves and others.

Refuse to cherish *you* and love for others is blocked. Self-love that says "me only" slates you for Self-defeat. Know that *self*-love and *Self*-love are opposites. The first is egocentric. The other is spiritual.

I can love from "hole" . . . neediness. Or I can love from "whole" . . . nonneediness. Only the latter is love.

Do you love from "hole" or "whole"?

Needy love clings, stifles, manipulates, possesses, controls. *Its focus is on intake.*

Nonneedy love affirms, gives freedom to grow and is "for" the Other. *Its focus is on outgive.*

Trouble comes when we confuse the two.

What I love determines *if* I love.

"Illness is blocked love . . . illness can be caused by non-acceptance or non-relinquishment of love."

PAUL BRENNER, M.D.

"Dishealth occurs when the mind refuses to relinquish self-deprecating thoughts."

PAUL BRENNER, M.D.

When we stop loving, we begin to die. If we have never loved, we have never lived.

Letting Go

"Resentment is the ultimate never-leaving-home."

FRITZ PERLS

Resent is from the French—to feel again. To resent—to refeel—has payoff.

Resentment lets us clutch injustice, not owning our part in it. With resentment we can punish Self and Other; have power; pad ourselves against pain. And we get to be right *and* unhappy.

Resentment substitutes for legitimate pain. However, substitutes for facing pain most often boomerang. For as long as we hold on to even justifiable resentment, we are irrevocably bonded to that pain.

Do you want to pay that price?

JOHN BRADSHAW (paraphrased)

Do you give resentment rent-free space in your mind? Many choose loyalty to past hurts. Where are your loyalties? What is their cost?

Nursing the grudge yields bitterness and anguish. It

wipes out today's joy. Each of us decides for ourselves whether to hold it.

———— ❦ ————

The only person's script I can change is my own. Yet, first, I need to be *willing* to do so.

———— ❦ ————

If I won't befriend me, I'll ask you for what I won't give me. But being on an emotional welfare line creates stress for all involved.

———— ❦ ————

"I am supposed to make it OK for everybody" is a killer. Constant "make nice" can wear you out. Be aware that some, no matter how you fix it, have a vested (unconscious) interest in sabotaging. Be aware you cannot "make nice" for them.

———— ❦ ————

Refuse to be caught up in other adults' refusal to take care of themselves. Caretakers end up getting taken.

———— ❦ ————

To worry is to hold on to the problem. Go for solution which may mean simply release.

———— ❦ ————

Some people appear to love but do not. They use the words; they exude the charm. But they lack the capacity to commit, to bond.

As children, such people grew up without experiencing commitment. Those around them were too committed to themselves. Be aware their old childhood pain is being acted out with you.

It is fruitless to invest emotionally, wish otherwise, resent or mourn the loss of such a relationship. The lesson is to face their reality. Sidestep the confusion of the camouflage. Understand they do not know how to live the language of love. Their honeyed words are for their needs alone. Ask yourself why you give them power in your life.

Using never has been, never will be love. It is their tragedy. Don't make it yours.

————◦◦◦————

Fear binds; detachment-with-love frees. Problems are as big as the energy I give them.

————◦◦◦————

Frozen expectations and beliefs are like gravity. To expand and grow, we need to continually be letting go. Otherwise we do not evolve in wisdom.

————◦◦◦————

Why is a relationship that drags you down often so hard to release?

Invariably there's an Inner Child need or belief involved. *Today's person is a symbol for one from the past.* Some common "hookers" that may glue us in the relationship are:

- the fear of not being attached to someone, anyone.

- the fear that a future relationship would not be better.

- the belief that being with anyone is better than being with one's Self.
- the need to do one's Self in; "I don't deserve a good relationship."
- the belief "If something's wrong, it must be my fault."
- the present negative allows us to stay with the pain known in childhood.

Doesn't make sense? Perhaps. But then emotional needs, dependencies and Inner Child beliefs do not make sense to our Rational Adult Self. Remember, it is the Irrational Child that clings to destructive relating. Not the Rational Adult Within.

———————

Imagine four banks on four corners. One has a sign reading, "No half dollars." You go to that bank and demand fifty-cent pieces. No matter how often they tell you they don't have them, you continue your demand. You bang your fist on the counter till it's bloody and bruised. Still what you want is not forthcoming. Even though three other banks are just outside, you make no move to go there. *You want your half dollars from this bank* which does not have them.

None of us would do this. Right?

Yet how often in relationships we ask for, demand a particular kind of coin that the Other truly does not have the capacity to produce.

We ask for caring; they cannot care. We ask for commitment; they cannot commit. We ask for sharing; they are noncommunicators. *Some have the coin you want; some do not.*

How long does it take to "get" this lesson? It takes as long as it takes. No one said letting go was easy.

Forgiving

Forgiving eases into place when we separate the person from the behavior. Reject the act, not the person.

———⸌⸍———

Do you believe in a statute of limitations for yourself? Others? In letting yesterday end last night?

On the other hand, in destructive relationships, it is essential to protect yourself. And to act accordingly.

———⸌⸍———

Forgiveness is not a luxury. It is a basic requirement for life. Nonforgiveness freezes energy into abscess. It bonds us tightly to its pain to crop out in physical and emotional dis-ease. Forgiveness includes self-forgiveness.

Destructive behavior comes from self-hatred. Self-put-downs are a form of nonforgiveness.

Wholeness, health, peace *require* we forgive.

———⸌⸍———

"Where there is a health problem, there is a forgiveness problem."

CATHERINE PONDER

———⸌⸍———

We need dreams to follow. But when we want others to fit our dreams, there is often a wake-up *mourning.*

———⸌⸍———

Will you choose to let a past painful relationship poison your willingness to reach out again?

As an infant you would never have walked if a hurtfull fall meant no more risking. Yet how many, after being burned once or twice, go for "never again" and withdraw.

If pain is pattern, look to your hidden needs. There may be an old childhood belief, "I don't deserve better," that drives you to pain-giving relationships. Or to provoking negative behavior from others. Or to fear of requiring respectful treatment. Give yourself permission to Self-protect.

Life is for living *and* learning. This means we risk, hurt, enjoy, share and love. With each connection we learn anew. *Hopefully.*

------❧------

Forgiveness yields the final freedom. Without it there is no healing. In eventually sending love's forgiveness, we empower and heal ourselves and add to the healing of the world.

Forgiving is for giving.

Healing

Feeling aloneness keenly is part of the process when a loved one leaves. This feeling needs working through, of course.

But then ask yourself, "How many do I know *in* a relationship that leaves them feeling lonely?"

Point: *Relationship per se is no guarantee against loneliness.* If I don't like me, I'll be lonely even with others around.

Loneliness ends when I enjoy me. Then when I'm with others, I bring my own gladness along.

An active faith and high self-esteem free us from loneliness. They are the ingredients that undergird healing.

Every day we make memories.

What kind of memories are you making? What are you choosing to do in your relationships? Are those choices pro- or anti-healing?

To seek to control, win, manipulate is to run from your Self. It is a denial that all you need is already within.

Affirm, "I am whole and complete," every moment. *Believing the positive heals.*

The mind is like a nest. What do you cradle there? Relational problems? None are free of their existence. Do you nest them? Or do they nest you?

Fear is what dwarfs you, not the problem.

The seed of solution lies at the core of every problem. Seeing yourself as a solver produces the power to surge through.

The solution may lie in reframing. When Edison's light-bulb failures mounted, he said he now knew many ways that did not work. Did he quit in defeat? No, he knew an answer awaited.

The worst only precedes the best. You alone decide what you nest: problems or solutions. Focusing on solutions gives the healing process the green light.

Are you on your knees for someone else's needs? Do you live life as an apology? If so, why?

We are meant to walk erect. Integrity asks that we heal stooped posture.

Give till it feels good. But never sacrifice integrity. As in all life, relationships require finding the balance point.

Small children think of their needs only . . . normal development.

Adult children think of their needs only . . . arrested development.

The hard reality is that if, as an adult, I run the Child script, my choices may dagger others as well as myself.

We are not healed till we set aside childhood scripts.

Obvious self-destructive choices: drugs, food, alcohol, promiscuity, overwork. Not so obvious self-destructive choices (more rampant): a series of refusals.

They are refusals to: Self-nurture, assume responsibility for Self, commit, face reality, consider impact on others, give up self-indulgence, give up overprotection, cease rebellion, passive resistance and/or overcompliance.

What are you choosing?

Personal healing is a matter of:

- awareness of the realities;
- willingness to stretch;
- decision to act and taking action;
- practice of the new behavior, attitudes.

———⟨∽⟩———

If you dislike yourself and wait for others to love you, they probably won't. If you affirm your Self, amazingly most others do too.

———⟨∽⟩———

Low self-esteemers fold around the belief "I am un-lovable." Yet they hunger for love. Classic double bind!

Deprived earlier, their Inner Child seeks to get from present relationships what it did not get then.

However, when life goes well, when low self-es-teemers get loving relationships, they have no con-scious choice but to sabotage. None of us can accept from the outer (love) what does not match the inner (the "I am unlovable" belief). When pluses come, low self-esteemers "must" destroy them to hold on to their "loser" belief.

Stopping this sabotage mandates a shift to self-affir-mation. Without it, no healing can come.

———⟨∽⟩———

Few of us shift from a particular stance without a pendulum to opposite before coming to middle ground.

If you've lived "doormat," you may swing to "ag-gressive-defensive" before you come to quiet assertion.

Healing lies in the balance point, not either extreme.

———⟨∽⟩———

When self-esteem is low, differences in those close threatens. When self-esteem is low, others' strengths make us feel one-down. Then we crouch or play "gotcha."

How much we can allow for differences in relationships is a statement of our own self-worth. The way out is to become a high self-esteemer. Only then do we fully love. And fully heal.

There is no question. The greatest healing force is Love.

Choosing Happiness

"I would be happy if only . . ." The death knell to contentment for adults. "Make me happy" doesn't work.

"Due me" expectations necessarily block peaceful relationships.

At the personality level, we all live with self-doubt, questioning, loneliness at times. How could it be otherwise when each of us is a first? To different degrees we all walk wounded. We do not differ here.

To freeze energy on past pain, however, blocks growing strength. Why not choose victory over defeat?

Claim courage. Trailblaze.

The various Anonymous programs have great wisdom for all. They teach: first things first; a day at a time; don't keep score; go for being happy over being right; easy does it; don't make mountains out of molehills; let go and let God. All part of respect for Self and Other.

———◦◦◦———

Never let another discourage you from fulfilling your dream. If you do, you give away your power, your choice and your happiness.

———◦◦◦———

Dr. Jack Canfield has pointed out that we can choose to live life as paranoids or inverse paranoids.

As paranoids we believe, "The universe is out to get me." Victim. Harvest: withdrawal, guardedness, *fear.*

As inverse paranoids, we believe, "The universe is out to do me good." Victory. Harvest: risk, joy, *love.*

What is your choice?

———◦◦◦———

Confronting with anger is often only an invitation to fight. Confronting by sharing your vulnerabilities is much more likely to build bridges.

———◦◦◦———

"My way or the highway" is one stance some people take. But self-will run riot and to heck with others never works in the long run. The day of reckoning always comes.

The only way that truly works is the High Way. And then *only* if lived.

———◦◦◦———

We keep the original of all we send out. The Other gets the carbon.

Resentment, fear, anger? Forgiveness, peace, love?

What originals are you filing? What price for their storage?

------∽------

When others send arrows, you can:

- hold the zap and hurt . . . not recommended.

- retaliate, which usually only escalates.

- share the effect on you and request a "cease."

- know that the Other is doing so *for* themselves, not *to* you. What belongs elsewhere is being hung on you.

- give them the space to do their arrow dance but refuse to let the barbs in . . . refuse to let another rain on your parade.

- visualize a plastic shield between you and the Other and "see" the arrow deflect short of you.

- seriously question why you remain if such darts are pervasive.

------∽------

Ask yourself, "What would I need to *give up* if I decided to be happy . . . in spite of?"

------∽------

"Most people are about as happy as they want to be."
                                                    ABRAHAM LINCOLN

------∽------

As we let go of the masks and roles, as we release self-doubt, as we clean up relationships, our Heart Light starts shining through. Then we begin singing our Heartsong. And life tastes very sweet.

LOSS

A LOVED ONE DIES

We know all people die. But not this one, please! Not yet! A bonding is cut. A finality exists. You are helpless against this loss. Perhaps the loved one was too young. Unfinished business may lie like a shroud. Mourning for what was, for what could have been, for what never was. Lost opportunity. Relief for their release from pain. But your pain cuts. The void of an emptiness no other can fill. No!

A RELATIONSHIP DIES

It happens all the time. But not *ours!* Why? What went wrong? Where did we fail? If only! Even if limited or downright negative, it was a connection, a bond and rootedness that was of our plans, our very grounding.

Losses are multiple: the person is gone, the role is gone, the lifestyle is gone, known stresses are gone, securities are gone, dependencies left dangling unattached.

If it is the marriage bond that breaks, depending on your religious beliefs, a sacred covenant is violated. The one who leaves may feel guilt for what has been done, perhaps pain for the Other's pain.

If it is the end of parenting, the "empty nest" closes a book forever. Those years cannot be recaptured. Or a dear friendship explodes. Regardless, when a valued connection is lost there is special pain. The Other, the connection, is gone. A glue that existed erodes. No!

A DREAM DIES

A belief about life or others, an illusion, a trust, a hope, a value is blown asunder. Work, health, finances, position, cherished goals evaporate. What we thought was, is not. What we counted on, trusted, believed in, disappears. Maybe betrayal. Raw, unadulterated pain. No!

No ritual supports the death of a dream, role, trust, friendship, health. Such pain is hardest of all. An intangible essential in your life is gone. No!

Some have a philosophy that allows an almost immediate acceptance of loss. They are convinced that any negative is but preface to a new positive. They believe that whatever happens is for the highest good; they accept almost without question. They genuinely do not resist. If true for you, this section is one you may want to skip or skim.

Others *think* they have that philosophy, but they simply *repress* grief and then physical and/or psychological problems erupt.

Most experience grief with loss. If you are in either of the last two groups, this section is for you.

Whenever loss shatters, the grief process triggers. You may know about the process, but when it happens, it is fresh no matter how often you've been there before.

Shock and denial: "This can't be happening." "It isn't real." "I don't believe it!"

Anger, rejection and guilt: "How could you do this to me (even if death is involved)?" "I want to flail out, to hurt back . . . at them, life, God." "I shouldn't feel this way." "It is totally unfair." "Why me?"

Bargaining: "I'll try harder . . ." "If only, I'll . . ."

Depression: "I feel hopeless, helpless, powerless to change what's happened." "How can I go on?" "What's the purpose?"

Disorientation: "I feel confused, scared, disconnected." "Nothing makes sense. Nothing feels solid." "I'm floundering." "I want to get away, go within, regroup." "I want to get my bearings . . . quickly."

Each of grief's steps has its own timing. Some experience the stages in sequence with varied intensity. At other times one stage flip-flops with another over and over. Sometimes the stages commingle. The greater the loss, the more the anguish and confusion. The dearer the cherishing, the more profound the grief. You ache for relief. It feels as if it will never end. You feel bereft.

If your particular loss is through divorce, your specific religious beliefs may mean that regardless of the legal paper, in your heart you remain very much married. Your former mate has turned from the covenant of your faith even though you have not. It is a time for active turning to your spiritual counselor.

To force any stage or try to skip over it through repression is to work against nature. It just does not work . . . regardless of others' expectations.

We can only surrender to the process. And avoid comparing our recovery with another's. We each have our own timing.

Recovery is not instant or short. Anniversaries, special songs, holidays, associations, retrigger what you thought was laid to rest . . . a year later . . . or two . . . or several. Yet we are designed to heal if we go *with* the process appropriately.

Remember, the tears that flow *out* are ones that heal. Those that flow *in* are those that abscess.

If your loss is fresh, you may want to wait a bit before reading this section. You hurt! That pain has loudest claim just now. Dawn may come slowly. On the other hand, you may wish to sample a few to see if some of these thoughts add balm.

To me, as an Air Force child, constant moving meant constant loss. No sooner established than gone. Roots in a family house, with extended clan, with predictability of place, friends, school, teachers, the known did not exist. Speech patterns from Ohio meant Yankee in Alabama; the Louisiana drawl was anathema in Kansas. All roots were in nuclear-nuclear family.

And then in my teens that known was blown apart. My beloved, never-sick-a-day father dropped dead without warning. He was so young; a high soul; it was not fair! My world spun. I remember waking the next morning furious that the sun dared to be so sparkling the day after his death. In my magical child thinking, because I was in total mourning, I felt that at least the day could have been cloudy. But life went on while I reeled inwardly for a good two years.

All goals then in place needed instant revision. My world went upside down as financially I was suddenly on my own. Yet I set out to get an education. There were graduate school days when twenty cents had to buy nine meals. But I hatched a marvelous plan.

I knew the Chinese often ate dry rice, drank water and felt full. I wasn't into dry rice, but in those days twenty cents bought two boxes of raisins. And water was free. I survived fine. All I knew was that I was determined to find a way no matter what.

In the ensuing years since my father's death, severe losses
—often coming in bunches—came from out of left field. Each
with no warning brought fresh shock, bewilderment, grief.
Some felt truly catastrophic at the time. But life went on.

Yet intermingled were great joys, fulfillments, soul-deep
satisfactions. The interesting awareness is that it was *those very
losses*, not the triumphs, that taught what I'd not known before. Each offered an invaluable lesson and asked me to
stretch . . . to become more whole. It seems that loss, ad-
versity, struggle fine-tune our instrument, much as we may
resist that route.

I remember asking my mother on her seventy-fifth birth-
day how she felt about reaching that age. Her eyes lit up as
she said, "Oh, Dorothy, I've learned more in the past five
years than I did in the first seventy!" And this woman had
suffered major losses early on. She knew personally that in
spite of devastating losses, each year brought sprouting and
newness.

Professionally, I have walked the path with those in deep
pain: death, catastrophic illness, divorce, loneliness, confusion, incest, abandonment, betrayal, substance abuse and so
many parenting pains. Walking with each taught me. Above
all, I learned that, reframed, pain does teach if we are open to
the lesson.

Paradoxically, each loss, grief, pain, fear is our *growing edge*.
We can *use* loss to expand our compassion, deepen our wisdom. Loss can empower us to come to Love.

To heal we are required to say goodbye to the old; hello to
the new. Final acceptance shifts energy to forward thrust.
Life can lose meaning when future obscures. Yet, to repeat,
that very pain when gone through can wake us to new, if we
allow it.

We can choose to block. To cling and refuse to budge. Yet

life asks for flexibility. It also asks us how fully we love. How fully we stay with our values in times of stress.

Falling short is part of the trip. The crucial issue is: Do we sell out? Or refuse to give up? Do we anchor in honor, integrity, decency and commitment to positive values?

Each day we answer these questions by how we live. It matters little that we falter. It does matter that we get up and correct.

This section is for those who vote for growth *because of* devastation. And the paradox is that it is this very process that can lead us to our Heartsong—the great purpose for which we were born, if we allow it. We each decide the verdict for how we handle loss.

What follows are sharings that have seemed to make a difference in using loss victoriously. They are offered as potpourri. If only a few give new focus, ease your way, their purpose will be fulfilled.

These are for keeping on your nightstand, best read sometimes in the wee hours. And reread. And again. They work better than tranquilizers or pain pills even if sometimes you might not like their flavor on first reading.

Before reading this section, remember:

Any loss is a threat. Your body gears for action—fight or flight. We are built to move at such times.

We moderns, however, too often "flee" into chemicals or sedentary activities. Or we may fight with our mouths and legal ploys. Large-muscle activity is too often neglected.

Two groups of people with high anxiety levels were given different programs. Group I had six months of psychotherapy. Group II was given a rigorous physical exercise program. After six months the exercise group was markedly less anxious than the therapy group.

So with loss, get physically active. Use those large muscles.

The end products of stress get worked off through exercise. Nature designed us to move at such times.

In addition, with loss it is important to:

- eat nutritious food;
- get adequate rest;
- put structure in your day (unstructured within makes this all the more urgent);
- make as few changes as possible—this one is enough;
- find social outlets;
- save time for activities that are *fun* for you.

When feelings run high, create a task, a project, a service with outward focus.

Depending on the severity of your loss, expect:

- disruption in sleep patterns;
- changes in appetite and sexual drive;
- lower frustration tolerance;
- trouble concentrating, remembering, learning new things;
- less resistance to physical illness;
- accident-proneness;
- increase in anxiety;
- a return to old coping strategies you may have given up years ago.

These are all part of the process. These too shall pass.

The Blow

Death, divorce, loss of all major types—each can feel like assault on your person. Respect your body's response. Deep wounds require attention. Others can help part of the way. But more rapid healing comes with tender, inner parenting from you to you. Gentle yourself. And lean on your faith.

No matter how old, each of us is a collection of every age we've ever been. With the stress of loss our Inner Needy Child almost always surfaces. It wants to go home to the safety of the womb or past loved ones. You are *not* being immature to want total enfoldment, comforting, protection, while you work through this grief.

Give yourself a break. Honor your Needy Child. Let it reach out to appropriate supports—physically and emotionally. But vote against any kind of anesthesia: drugs, alcohol, food. They only start another round of problems, bringing at best only temporary relief. At enormous cost. When your Hurting Inner Child feels the safety of Inner Nurturing, it will go with you secure in the future.

"I can't go on, can't function without the lost one." A common, common part of grief. You may need to stay with that belief during the initial loss period. But soon remind yourself that you functioned *with* the Other here because you *believed* they gave you the *power* to cope. But *you did the actual coping.* You produced the power

within yourself *with that belief.* It was your belief that
provided the energy.

Once you "get" this idea and believe in your capacity, you have it made. You can cope without leaning on
others—comfortable as that was. Lean instead on your
faith.

From infancy on we all seek to make sense to ourselves, of others and what's around. Definite rooting
keeps us secure. Is it any wonder, then, when the
known falls away that the place of suspension, the de-
geared space, spins us? We lose all bearings. The anti-
dote is faith. It makes this "I don't know" tolerable
while we seek to re-gear.

If ever there is a time when faith is needed, it is during and following any major loss.

Truth . . . wisdom . . . seems to lie dead center of
paradox.

When you take the courage to go directly into the
emptiness of loss, you see, feel afresh in time.

Pay sharply focused attention *to that emptiness.* Enter
the void. Sit still in it and just "be" with it. This stage is
fallow time . . . part of the process of grief.

You'll find yourself wanting to reminisce, to go back
over, to put the pieces together. Honor this stage. Remi-
niscing helps put the past in perspective . . . to tie up
the package . . . to let go. You are on the edge of a
turning point.

Withdrawal comes before reentry. When you face
into the emptiness, it disappears.

Loss is compounded when friends don't understand the enormity of your pain. It hurts when they fail to give the particular support you so badly want. They bring flowers, logic and cheery masks when your deepest need is for a listening heart.

Many reasons backdrop this phenomenon. Rarely is it lack of caring. Many are so busy with their own concerns they cannot hear yours. Others feel helpless, so pull away. Some feel scared—it could happen to them. Others don't hear the call. Some, never having experienced your kind of loss, simply do not understand.

Actually, our culture does not teach us how to be with others in their pain. "Cheer 'em up," "Avoid the topic." Anything but deal openly with the wound.

Your best resources are others who've been there. And those few who feel free to walk with you in that pain. Reading materials, support groups, helping professionals and prayer round out the network you need. Just remember, you do *need* support, even if only from one or two.

A sad reality is that many who have not walked your pain will expect you to shape up fast. "Be strong," you'll be told.

Don't push your river. Claim your right to heal as nature designed. You will have your own particular timetable. Honor it.

How long this pain? This hurt? This confusion? It takes as long as it takes. To stop resisting what is. To stop taking counsel with fear. To activate hope. These take *time*.

———❦———

A killer in stress is "either-or." We need to switch to "and." Loss is crisis *and* invitation.

———❦———

Loss spawns helpless. Helpless spawns fear. The only certainty is change. Physical matter and all life are in constant flux. But Changeless Spirit lies within. The great paradox, of course, is that we *do* need to lose to find. If we hold fast to That-which-never-changes, loss speeds us to new.

———❦———

Loss. A stop point? Or a pause point? Coffin? Or catapult? We each choose which. Loss is life's demand that we stretch.

———❦———

Every loss is a choice point. We go or grow through it. The latter is the only victory. And each challenge met only strengthens our foothold in life.

———❦———

Venting negative feelings *is part of constructive healing.* Yet it is wise to choose carefully: certain persons, certain times. Few will hang out with you for long. If you stay stuck—bitter, inturned—more loss comes.
Others steer clear.

———❦———

To have known structure crumble, to have what was counted on and trusted forever lost, is to be propelled into void. To deny this scary place is insult.

———❦———

Crumbling, of necessity, *precedes* all new growth. Wilting *precedes* taking hold in all nature. Seed casings break; cocoons split; placentas are discarded *before* never imagined beginnings flower.

Reframed, loss becomes gateway. We each choose how we see.

———⌘———

"Awfulizing" is part of the grief process. Yet it *is* resisting what happened. Acceptance comes gradually, in spurts . . . fragilely held at first. Yet hope for the future heals.

What Loss Teaches

Among other things, loss teaches that there are no guarantees. It teaches that periodically we will be required to let go. It reminds us that we increase our vulnerability if we do not accept this fact.

———⌘———

Overly intense abandonment feelings from today's loss often come from an earlier abandonment whose grief was never laid to rest . . . not worked through.

———⌘———

Letting go of "how it should be" where loss is concerned begins the bridge to healing.

———⌘———

It is important to remember that I cannot get near the buzz of another's saw (their destructive script) and not get hurt.

With certain losses we need to do a reality check: "What did I *actually lose?*" When looked at squarely, there may be no substance to miss. The loss was unfulfilled promise. Realistically, it was an "unsatisfactory" in our life.

Mourning for that? Of course. But for how long? We cannot *not* deal with reality . . . eventually.

Did you lose substance or promise? Reality or illusion?

In retrospect, some losses are spelled G A I N S. Better is on its way. Losing that job, that role, that connection, may open up greater opportunity for new parts of you to unfold. It takes courage to hope. Fear is easy.

Yet with each loss some newness begs to be born. Recall, loss is stepping-stone or tombstone, always depending on our attitude.

Which will yours be?

If my question is, "How can this happen to me?" distress and anguish follow. If my question is, "What lesson can I learn from this?" growth and renewal follow. What is your question?

Yesterday's disaster is today's teacher if we linger past the pain to learn the lesson.

Fleas in a lidded jar soon accept that limit. They jump short of the top even after the lid is removed. If you believe your loss limits you forever, you'll reduce your efforts. However, when you *know* you are limitless, regardless of outer circumstances, you are free to find a way.

What we believe, we live.

━━━━━━━◦◦━━━━━━━

If you've been devastated by another's betrayal, you try to make sense out of chaos. Be aware that others' early conditioning and low self-worth cause them to pull you into the service of their needs. They may say the words of love but act otherwise. When their masks crack, you find they live a style totally foreign to you. Realize the Other *is* Other and they speak another language.

Walk *your* path. Be aware. Again, ask what you have literally lost. Illusion and pain? One whose values are alien to yours?

━━━━━━━◦◦━━━━━━━

Fear blocks learning the lesson. Life asks us to play ball. It asks us to master the hold. And then life asks that we let go. We literally scare ourselves out of the ball game if we fear letting go. We live in Scarce City . . . scarcity.

━━━━━━━◦◦━━━━━━━

"She should have seen the doctor sooner." "He should never have done that." You may be totally right.

Yet, after quality mourning, to keep clinging to the "shoulds" draped around that loss does block healing.

━━━━━━━◦◦━━━━━━━

Until fully grieved and released, old pain shadows and distorts today.

———⊷⊷———

When dark spiral whirls you down, when you cannot see ahead, start counting your gratitudes. How could this "terrible" be worse? It is amazing what lamps turn on.

Like oil and water, glad and unhappy simply don't mix.

———⊷⊷———

The lost illusion is hard to surrender. Yet we can trust what *is* more than the dream.

When your expectation is irrational in the light of reality, *your obsession is on the unreal.* And you continue to obsess *until you drop that unreal illusion.*

———⊷⊷———

After honoring grief's process, listen to the victims of life-threatening disease. They teach invaluable secrets:

"I was jammed into reappraisal."

"Time is limited; so I go for joy; quality is what matters, not quantity."

"Meaning comes from family, friends, loving, outreach."

"Possessions don't nurture."

"If I must compare, I think of someone less fortunate."

No question. Serious disease can unleash reframing. Why wait for cancer or heart attack to reframe? Do it now.

———⊷⊷———

"The Other's been deceptive and cruel and ripped me off!" To be demolished pains so.

Yet to *expect* the emotionally crippled to act as if they are not is irrational. Denying the Other's hang-ups leaves you dependent on proven instability.

Was the dream that one day the Other would wake? Such dreams can become nightmares. Only spiritual awakening can heal some people.

———— ❧ ————

To automatically assume others play by your rules can lead to disappointment, pain.

———— ❧ ————

Why is not so important as *that* it is. The former mires us. The latter lets us move to new.

———— ❧ ————

Every loss creates imbalance. Yet all forward movement requires we briefly forgo the balance place.

Remember your first two-wheeler ride? It took conscious effort and constant correcting to keep balanced. Recovery from loss is no different. Uncharted takes us off balance. Moment-by-moment readjustment is asked till we get the hang of the new terrain.

———— ❧ ————

To overcome takes effort. There's no free lunch. Disuse weakens; struggle strengthens. Give yourself great mental bouquets for scaling this hurdle. Stay on course.

———— ❧ ————

In spite of its disadvantages, the loss of a symbiotic relationship (strong-weak, responsible-irresponsible)

can rip you apart. Part of "you" is gone. Be aware you
may seek to replace your other "half" with more of the
same. This sets the stage for future pain.

Loneliness comes when you lose connection with the
valued. Of course. But when loneliness persists after its
time, consider these issues: Are your expectations real-
istic? Do you fear further hurt? Lack needed social
skills? Turn in, not out? Retreat with excessive sensitiv-
ity and lack of self-worth?

We all need bondings . . . social networks. Solution:
Admit your loneliness to yourself and look to your expectations. Whittle them down to fit reality. Get involved. To have a friend, be one. Reach out rather than
waiting to be reached out to.

GIVE.

We never lose a true love. Their impact on our lives is
irrevocably with us always. Remember that as you
mourn your dear one. They are always as close as your
memory. They have left a precious piece of themselves
with you forever.

The most frequent earthquakes are inner ones. They
are needed to break up a belief "foundation" so that a
better one may be built. Losses are emotional earthquakes of varying degrees of magnitude. The greater
the intensity, the larger the possibility for more funda-
mental reconstruction to take place.

The High Cost of Resistance

Water is wet. Rocks are hard. What is, *is*. *Pain comes when we resist reality.*

Resistance traps energy. Resist not evil or it holds you in its power. Is the lost your magnificent obsession? Cruel question, but worth considering. Prolonged "I can't get over it" may mean "I don't want to." Resistance costs a bundle. It does not come cheap.

Why this choice when recovery is at stake?

———❦———

Fear of death and aging wipe out enjoying life today.

———❦———

Retirement can be a special form of loss. No less painful, especially if you tie your identity to your job. Yet as Paul Bragge said in his nineties, "To rest is to rust."

Never retire; only switch. Meaningful service needs *you*. Start today.

———❦———

Youth, being a state of mind, can never be lost. The young have vitality, flexibility, a sense of adventure and curiosity. They thrust forward, see freshly and greet life with spontaneous enthusiasm. They are active, full of wonder and hope. They believe in possibility.

Those of many years who have these qualities are forever young . . . and a joy to be around. Those of few years who lack such qualities are old. As Maurice

Chevalier said, "Never resent growing old. Think of the millions who are denied the privilege."

Years do not steal youth. Attitudes do. Eternal youth is yours for the embracing.

———————

No loss is so great as the refusal to love your Self. No abandonment is more cruel than the abandonment of Self. For when we come from self-doubt, self-hate or self-delusion, invariably we refuse to love others as they are. We cannot love without strings. We cannot love unconditionally. We do not stand in Love.

Resisting self-affirmation slates you for pain. And it is a stressor that sets you up for physical and emotional disease.

———————

Fear of Self-sufficiency—wholeness—can cause us to cling to friendships that work against us. Ask yourself what price you pay.

Clingers often get knife points, not Brownie points. Fear of loneliness can create the cling. But what have you lost when a relationship asks that you not grow? Gives you no support? Asks you to pull all the weight? Features one-sided commitment?

Relationships that ask you to be untrue to your Self cut into the fabric of Self. You were not created for that.

———————

Moment by moment we continually say "yes" or "no" to life and love by our choices. By our attitudes. By our actions.

———————

Healing comes with acceptance. Repeatedly, life propels us to release, surrender attachments, beliefs.

To resist loss is ultimately to resist life. Life is and always has been constant flux. Loss weaves its way through the very fabric of life. Status quo is purely temporary. Yet how we cling to it.

We do not fully say yes to life until we say yes to death. Yet we humans *do resist that life and loss are a package deal.*

Reframing Loss

"When it gets darkest, the stars come out,
When the bee steals from a flower, it also
fertilizes that flower."

CHARLES A. BEARD

Darkness, of course, is only the absence of light. We each have the power and responsibility to throw on the Switch. Gray does not forever stay . . . unless some part in us gets mileage from it. You know the popular saying, "Turn the lemons into lemonade."

It works!

Healing is finding the balance between honoring the dignity of your pain, riding with it right to its core. But not obsessing, wallowing or embracing its stepchildren: bitterness, withdrawal and defeat.

"Death is not extinguishing the light,
   But putting out the lamp because the dawn has
      come."

RABINDRANATH TAGORE

———◦∞◦———

Locking on to negatives is a contract with gloom.
Locking on to positives is a contract with joy. To heal,
give yourself permission for joy. Revel in the good, the
pluses of what was and is.

———◦∞◦———

"Men are disturbed, not by things, but by the views
which they take of them."

EPICTETUS, A.D. 100

Rephrased: We may have no control over the event,
but we have ultimate control over our reaction to the
event.

Much modern research is showing we *do* have control
over many events by the kinds of behaviors, expectations and mind pictures we create.

Regardless, when self-esteem is high, we refuse to be
defeated. We find a way to *overcome* and re-create good.

Crossing the Healing Threshold

Read this as whisper when healing is almost complete. Some truths hurt to read. We want to deny them.

In grief, the Inner Child weeps because it cannot have
what it wants. It cries, "Don't take my loved one."
"Give me back my security." "Leave me my attach-
ment." "Don't destroy my dream." "Don't ask me to

grow whole all by myself." "I don't want to go into the uncharted."

Quietly naming the reality of the Child's plea can finalize healing. At that healing point—slowly—we release the cry.

And then we stand on threshold. We can remain needy and seek outside ourselves. Or we can turn to the Inner Child, enfold and comfort it. We can reassure it that *we* are its future. We can contract to take excellent care of it. And proceed to do so . . . daily. Finally we can take it to the Ultimate Healer, the One who always carries and supports.

——————

The surest eraser of the ache in loss is to reach out and give.

——————

If one approach doesn't work, try another . . . and another . . . and another. There *is* a way.

——————

After quality mourning, further looking back becomes going back. Healing asks that we look forward and up.

——————

A condolence letter to a man whose wife of forty years had died: "Congratulations for forty years of marriage to one of the finest women I've ever known."

Insensitive? Maybe not. Attitudinal repositioning is a gift . . . a key to unlock the healing process.

——————

We are asked eventually to transcend the grief, pain, rage, might-have-beens, regrets, dreams, plans. And by that transcendence, we enlarge our compassion and our wisdom.

———————

It takes *strength* to let go.

———————

Do you give up (defeat)? Or do you give up (release)?

———————

Loss is like going through the birth canal. You are squeezed, pushed, disoriented, thrust from known. It is pitch dark.

But you are in process. You will be asked to function quite anew. The impossible dream lies ahead. The Light does come.

———————

Survivors against all odds invariably have a vehement *desire* to make it, *conviction* they will and active *faith*.

———————

Old Zen saying: "Grab hold *lightly;* let go *tightly.*"

———————

An essential for healing is to release regrets. What you did or did not do; did or did not say. Part of healing is to forgive yourself. And the Other. And life. To fail to forgive impedes moving freshly ahead.

———————

It is foolish to justify. It is wise to seek healing.

———————

Was it I—my person—who was betrayed? Or my dream, my trust, my expectation?
Only *I* can betray *me*.

———————

"Life is the childhood of our immortality."
GOETHE

———————

"I lift up mine eyes unto the hills. From whence cometh my help? My help cometh from the Lord."
PSALMS 121:1

———————

There is no death. There is only transition.

Singing Your Song

The Heartsong—the Center Purpose for your life—becomes clear when you:

- listen deeply within;
- follow that intuition that directs you to purpose. Every loss can, if we tune in, bring that purpose into clearer focus. Remember, you are *not* here by accident. You are here by design.

You will know you are about that purpose when:

- doing it feels good, gives a sense of personal meaning;

- it does no harm to Self or Other;
- it gives to Life; it is outflow.

Bringing purpose to fruition for some involves rigorous self-discipline and sweat (agony and ecstasy). For others it just flows. Regardless, set your goal, actively pursue the steps needed to meet it. Let no person, no thing, discourage you from what you know you have to offer.

Remember: your Heartsong will push from within as deep desire. The word "desire" is from the French: "desire" . . . *of the Father*. With sustained and careful listening some deep sense within will tell you if your desire is "of the Father." If so, follow it. Then void disappears; loneliness is not an issue; loss is challenge.

Out of the ashes, the new arises . . . as planned.

LIFE

L IFE! Tough yet fragile, that precious energy pulsates through each of us for a particular number of days.

Each unique. Yet each alike in having the freedom to choose. Each alike in needing to love and be loved.

As Eric Berne said, "Every baby is born a prince or a princess and then people and life come along and turn them into frogs. Our job is to turn them back into princes and princesses." The good news is that we can midwife ourselves into whole, loving human beings. We *can* come into our own goodness.

When we do so, we shift from old conditioning, old messages that told us we were unlovable. We can each become a love-link that adds to a positive future for humankind.

Emerson said, "The unexamined life is not worth living." We can each choose to examine our lives and correct when we miss the mark. Not to do so is to live life blind.

Emerson also said, "Imitation is suicide." We were not born to cancel out our gift—our originalness—by imitating or comparing. Yet look at the energy spent on being like all others.

We all search for meaning and direction in spite of many detours. The good news is that we can use life itself as a guidepost to wholeness, love and purpose.

Everywhere we see-hear of crisis, trauma, problems, fear. Yet these very negatives can be used as fuel for positive change. The fabric of our nation is being torn by breakdowns in its basic institutions: marriage, family, church, schools. And we know that each institution is only as strong as its weakest link.

To right wrongs, we each need to use our energy constructively. And we cannot go wrong when we ground in Love's principle.

The common thread uniting all who are destructive to Self and Others is low self-esteem. We each bring our own degree of self-worth to family, school, workplace, community, nation. To the extent that we increase our self-worth, we become builders rather than destroyers.

The collection of life lessons that follows is shared with the hope that they may trigger your own life's examination. And, if appropriate, some will add to your own learnings. Hopefully, the ideas will enrich your journey toward renewal, wholeness, love. Then your path ahead will be steadier and more clearly focused.

Each of life's specific seasons offers new wisdoms. *We* decide whether we let this unfolding take place. You and I touch countless others every day. How we vote to live life makes a dramatic difference. We make others the beneficiaries or victims of how we stand in life.

May you decide to use life's lessons so that each day becomes an adventure in trust, caring and love. May your walk in life *add to* Love by how you live it.

Maxims

Life is a firm teacher. We are required to learn lessons. Once one is mastered, we are presented with the next one. Discouraging?

Not if we know that each one mastered brings new muscle to climb higher. And the higher the climb, the grander the view.

———❧———

Rose gardens without thorns? Happiness without pain? Completeness without doubt? Not so.

———❧———

Hard-to-say "nos" compound to win long-range treasure. Saying "yes" to constructive choices and "no" to destructive forces bring intentions to flower. We play Saboteur or Supporter. Yes? No? Which will it be?

How we experience life reveals our answer.

———❧———

We hear that what you don't know won't hurt you. Not necessarily so. In life, growing free is not possible for those who refuse to become *aware* that they are not free of old conditioning. Life requires we give up the no longer appropriate beliefs of low self-esteem if we want to be whole.

———❧———

In the beginning was the Word. And the Word was made flesh.

In childhood, the spoken/unspoken words of others

built the flesh of your self-picture. You borrowed the view of Others and called it "Me."

Adulthood's task is to re-create. How do you talk to you about you? What kind of self-talk diet are you on? Self-worth shrivelers? Or Self-worth builders?

Your self-talk creates the flesh of your self-image. Your body is a walking autobiography. How you live life is a personal summary of your private self-talk.

———————

Our destiny is cast by what we add after "I am." "I am inadequate" or "I am one with success" makes your life potently different.

———————

You've heard of postnasal drip. Now know of "postcortical" drip: that litany of self-put-downs. A backdrip against which we live our days. "I'll probably goof," "I am afraid," "I can't do it alone," wipe out being empowered.

Affirming "I have what it takes," "I am enough to scale the challenge," is the language winners use. Carefully guard what you etch in your mind.

Do you inwardly speak for or against your Self?

———————

As infants, we rely heavily on intuition. Later we are taught to turn from that source. Trust your intuition. It is rarely off-beam. And can save you from much stress if you heed it.

———————

If I reject my shadow side, I'll reject yours. Acknowledging our own shadow gives us tolerance for others.

But choosing not to act out those frailties shifts us from the Child script to the Adult one.

If there is not room for failure in your life, there is not room for risking or growth.

What you *can* do is more important than what you *cannot* do.

A wise person said, "Never ask a question that you don't want the answer to."

What questions do you ask? Not ask? Why?

"Sometimes life's shadows
   are caused by our standing
   in our own sunshine."

RALPH WALDO EMERSON

Facing Fears

If we call a spade a spade, we refuse to duck away from hard reality. You may not like the sound of this one, but . . .

Fear of responsibility comes from lack of self-confidence—the belief that I can't do it, might make a mistake, might be rejected if I risk.

No question. Low self-esteemers come from fear. Their inner self-picture is jammed with negatives and limitations about themselves.

Fear of responsibility is the decision *not* to grow free. *Fear of success is the offspring of fear of responsibility.* We want the prize but refuse to work for it. We want instant gratification. And may scapegoat others and life for our failure to get it. We don't want to take full responsibility for our daily lives. Avoid responsibility and growth stops. And the loser script plays on.

Develop the attitude of "So what?" to rejection and failure when you risk. No one goes from A to Z in one leap. No one. Once you believe in yourself, you are determined to make it no matter how many times you run into roadblocks.

Courage *is* the opposite of fear.

———————

Fear is faith—in the negative.

———————

Negative thinking burns energy. Positive thinking channels energy.

———————

The more we hang out with fears, the larger they become. The more we hang out with hopes, the larger they become. Which do you give power to?

———————

A mere match dispells darkness. If one goes out, you strike another. A mere hope dispells despair. If one goes out, claim another. Claim hope and you claim light. Why not?

———————

You up anxiety if you stay with "what if" followed by a dire thought. Do you want to scare yourself that way?

What we picture we get. If we focus on a dire one, we get fear. If we focus on anger, we get hate. Picture light, we get peace; picture love, we get love. What pictures are you hanging in the gallery of your mind?

Responsible is not responsible until *acted* upon. Big talk, little do, *doesn't* do.

When I acknowledge a weakness, I know where my growing needs to take place.
Each weakness I deny conquers me. Pinioned there forever, I am never free.

Oysters use the sand-grain irritant to make the treasured pearl. Life asks this of you and me.

If you cling to the Dependent Child stance, you'll seek Caretakers. And resent them. The amount of dependency equals the amount of hostility. Life is too short for such.
Growing up means giving up dependency . . . taking charge of your own life.

If you are true to your Self, not everyone will like you or approve. If you like You, then you accept that. Otherwise, the game is chameleon.

———◦❦◦———

Beneath hate or coldness is fear. And that fear is past, frozen, unexpressed grief.

———◦❦◦———

I do others a favor when I shift the magnifying glass off them. I do myself a favor when I pick up a mirror. In both cases it helps to see afresh with the eyes of Love.

———◦❦◦———

Victorious living does not come from good fortune's smiles. It comes rather from victory over dark.

———◦❦◦———

We all know or hear of people who in spite of the harshest extremes keep their spirits high. We admire. How do they do it? They search for the plus, give to others and keep faith.

Why not *decide* to do the same? The world needs your example.

———◦❦◦———

To seek happiness directly is to miss it. To give it to others is to find it. Live in Love.

———◦❦◦———

Thoreau said, "Only that day dawns to which we are fully awake."

To be fully awake is to know who you truly are . . .

a miracle of creation. The choice: awake-alive; asleep-dead.

Choose life!

The greatest intimacy comes not from sex. Rather it comes from sharing your inner world with another.

Mask, stay safe and be lonely. Reveal, risk censure, chance connection.

Psychological connecting is what intimacy is all about.

So many are touch-hungry. The need is for more than the hug. The real "fold-in" comes with empathic understanding—whether you joy or you pain. It cures loneliness.

Hearing is healing when it comes from the heart. Shared joy is expanded; shared pain reduced.

Without touching, life becomes solitary confinement. Do you sentence your Self? Or the Others?

As a child it was not so. As an adult it is so: The more vulnerable we are, the less vulnerable we become.

Do you vote for the power of love over the love of power? You cannot not vote.

As you stand in life's polling booth, it is wise to remember: power corrupts; love empowers.

The answer to your question, "Is this for or against me and/or the Other?" tells whether you sign a contract to avoid pleasure or go for joy.

———⟨∞⟩———

Low self-esteemers cannot know joy. If you find joy hard to come by as an attitude, best look to changing the negative beliefs you hold about You.

———⟨∞⟩———

When you embrace your opposite qualities, when you accept the finiteness of this lifetime's stay, you make each day count. You go for life's sweeteners: wonder . . . joy . . . appreciation . . . humor . . . outreach . . . commitment . . . Love. Too busy is no excuse. Make time.

Why settle for less?

Confronting the "Big Lie"

Do you unconsciously base your life on the Big Lie . . . "I am unlovable"? You do so if you believe you are what you do.

We all want to be loved aside from performance. Yet so many feel they have to earn love . . . "I am lovable if . . ." They live with the perform-or-perish blueprint.

If water from a hose is dirty, you clean up the water's source. You don't fuss with the hose. You do not confuse water with hose.

When your attitudes or behavior are off, clear them up. They come from and through you. *But they are not you.*

Confusion comes with this fusion . . . the source of so much pain.

----------⟨∽⟩----------

Far too much energy flows into this Big Lie. When my lovability is conditional, when my behavior falls short, *I* am rejectable. So I create

- a Pretend Self that will be loved;
- a Powerful Self that will be saluted;
- a Perfect Self that cannot be faulted;
- a Wrathful Self that scares others off.

But none of these ploys gives peace. Stop. Think. *God did not create you to put that Creation down.* If He loves you, you *are lovable.*

Claim your birthright! Erase the Lie! Once you do, it is easy to clear the water flowing from you.

----------⟨∽⟩----------

It is the rare person with no hang-ups. If I play my hang-ups, I give them power over me. If I learn from them, I take charge of my life.

----------⟨∽⟩----------

My Inner Critic will keep score *against* me. My Inner Nurturer refuses that trap. I need to know where I need to grow. Of course. But then I need to keep score *for* myself. If you're not on your own team, who will be?

----------⟨∽⟩----------

We can only change our future if we change destructive, irresponsible attitudes, beliefs and actions today.

----------⟨∽⟩----------

We are as stressed as the secrets we keep. If behavior needs hiding, don't do it.

Secrets corrode the keeper.

———⟨∽⟩———

High self-esteemers refuse to violate honor, integrity, commitment and Love. Low self-esteemers come from a script that causes them to intend and promise but weave away from delivery.

Values are the soil in which we grow and die. We each choose our own soil. Part of high self-esteem is choosing to anchor in positive values.

Capitulation dishonors Love.

Exercise Your Choice

Ever notice how a pup greets the day? You can consciously decide to "puppy" in life. It only requires a particular mind-set . . . a simple gear shift in choice.

Make a good day!

———⟨∽⟩———

Laughter makes me chemically different within. Part of emotional health is to be able to laugh at myself and life. No greater tonic.

———⟨∽⟩———

Children are marvelous teachers. You can be willing to see as a child sees . . . with freshness and wonder. Joy is a daily choice. You make it happen.

Give yourself permission to joy.

———⟨∽⟩———

"Reach for a sweet experience instead of a sweet," Sid Simon says. The sweetest one will be to give a piece of your caring away.

———∞———

It is my responsibility to protect my life energy. I have only so much to spend each day. I can choose not to waste it on games, proving, secrets, hurting Self/Others.

Channeling energy into Love actually produces energy.

———∞———

"I don't want to do it; it's hard." "I'd rather have the immediate pleasure." "I'm not in the mood." "I fear the outcome." One blueprint for life.

The price for avoidance, however, inflates over time. Commitment to hard decisions (self-discipline) *avoids* "avoid." And gives long-range payoff.

———∞———

Avoidance is a-void-dance. Are you dancing a void? Why?

———∞———

What you want determines *how* you travel.

———∞———

Tightly held childhood beliefs of what "it" is supposed to be like can wreck adult living. What "should" be may not be what is.

Life *satisfaction* comes when we *up* our contact with *reality* (of Other, Self, situation) and keep our *expectations* in line with that reality. Not to check what you expect with what is real sets you up for disappointment, pain.

Upsets are born within. Upsets are setups we create when our expectations go unmet.

No amount of resistance changes the past. Spilled milk cannot be unspilled. We clean the spill and avoid repetition. Yes, yesterday did end last night!

A career of "no" to me, "yes" to you is martyrdom. A career of "yes" to me, "no" to you is narcissism. Both *will barbwire.*

Overindulgence is not the point. But neither is deprivation. Finding the balance is daily challenge.

The path *out* of pain is often found by going *into* pain. It hurts but can then be laid to rest. It is done.

Life is not about arrival but about the trip.

Dreams (goals) give points to head for. Dreams (expectations) can stand between you and happiness.

Check out your dreams. Are they motivators? Or barriers?

Naming Your Game

How do you live life? As a

- workhorse?
- procrastinator?
- betrayer?
- affirmer?
- learner?
- gloomer?

- computer?
- prover (what point)?
- target?
- adventurer?
- forgiver?
- love-er?

Just for fun, consciously try on some of these different hats for a day. Amazing game. Eye-opener.

———

If I say I am humble, I am not.

———

Did you ever stop to think: condemning ourselves for what we do can be a cop-out for cleaning up our act?

———

No one can diminish you without your consent.

———

Long-term happiness does not come from a short-term fix.

———

Self-pity multiplies depression. Self-respect and self-care ease it. Highs pass; lows pass. Life is ebb and flow.

———

Once you go to the core of your fears, you often find they are but boogeymen.

Amelia Earhart said, "Courage is the price that life exacts for granting peace." Courage springs from faith. Courage is the vehicle of change. Courage brings you to the new.

When you are fearful, ask, "What's the worst that can happen?" Is that worst really so insurmountable? When fear comes, do a reality check.

Set your goals. Do your footwork to bring your promise to flower. See, feel, claim that it is so. First you treat; then move your feet. Then release to Grand Design.

Do, know, let go, let God.

Faith, a positive attitude and the willingness to expend effort are needed to reach goals.

Sometimes

- slow is fast
- fast is slow
- easy way out is hard way in
- hard way out is easy way in
- losing is winning
- winning is losing.

It is important not to confuse the two.

A positive attitude is seeing the diamond through the dust—in others, in life. But *overlooking* the reality of the dust can trip you up.

Until we hit enough pain, we are not willing to deal with the real issues. Pain is life's way of requiring that we face certain realities, learn the particular lesson, change the belief, fear, attitude, shift energy to singing our unique song.

Running from pain never works. It flies with you to flare when you stop. Stuffed feelings build inner steam to explode into symptoms and torn relationships.

Appropriate dealing with pain (left over from childhood or happening now) is the only way that does work.

Who and what am I refusing to love?
Where am I refusing to act?
How am I refusing to serve?
Why?

Holding back dams energy in. Stagnation . . . decay. Releasing streams energy forth. Vitality . . . life.
Refusals, hold-backs set you up to live life dead.

If you won't give yourself permission to be playful, who else will? Do you make your Playful Child a closet relative?

If you give yourself excessive permission to play, the Inner Child runs rampant. Consequences either way. As always, balance is the key.

Living New Choice

What you *believe* to be true about you acts as a filter to affect your *choices*. Those choices lead to *experiences* that support your beliefs. Negative beliefs about your Self lead to loser choices and painful experiences.

Even if at first you do not believe the positives, why not give them a try? "Act as if" and before you know it, you'll be on a benign cycle. It is called the self-fulfilling prophecy. And it works!

In short, what you *believe* for you, you *say* for you, you *choose* for you, is *so* for you.

In this sense we all succeed.

———❧———

What do you want engraved on your tombstone?

- "Here lies a collector of possessions"?
- "Here lies a wielder of power and status"?
- "Here lies a victim"?
- "Here lies a faultfinder"?
- "Here lies a people-user"?
- "Here lies a lover of life and people"?

———❧———

If you believe death is the final negative, your life clusters around denial and survival. You seek immortality through power, sensate pleasure and possessions. Then you cannot live Love.

If you believe death is but transition, a returning Home, you let your flame flow in Love's bright light. Then you truly live.

You are dead center of choice points when guilts come up. You can:

- make amends/restitution and *keep repeating*—sure way to fatten the guilt collection. The payoff is that you stay with the belief that you are a loser. This is the low self-esteemer's favorite pastime;

- make amends/restitution and *change behavior*— productive because of positive growth. This is the high self-esteemer's choice;

- turn guilts into *anger/rage* at the Other, whom you see as responsible for making you feel guilty or causing your behavior (innocent victim). This is the low self-esteemer's choice;

- check guilt out with reality and find that the guilt is the result of an old message ("You should feel awful about this") that has *no basis in fact today*. This is the high self-esteemer's choice.

What are you choosing?

Perfectionists have trouble with love. They tally "fall-shorts" and look for the hole. Like war, perfectionism is dangerous for people and other living things.

Why choose it? You are lost before you start.

———⋘———

What you tell yourself is under your control. Try thinking a dire thought. Note its effect on you. Now think a glad thought and note your change.

Remember, you choose your thoughts.

———⋘———

"Safety does not lie in staying safe in the world."

JANIS OLSEN

———⋘———

Anesthetize pain and you anesthetize joy.

———⋘———

Choose to sit in the feeling. Feel the hurt. You will survive. And heal. And stretch. And grow. More hurts will come. But you've proved to yourself you can overcome.

The alternative is walling off, copping out or covering up . . . self-imposed prisons.

———⋘———

Not until my walk matches my talk can you count on me.

Opening Your Options

When "I've always done it this way" becomes my "have to" blueprint, I am its slave.

Frozen-on-one-option (script usually created in childhood) wipes out flexibility and newness. Rigid prevents growing free.

———————

Constantly remind yourself that to give up doing what isn't working in your life requires changing your belief system. Remember, it's old *beliefs* that need fixing. Not *you*. You couldn't change your Self if you tried. You can only change your beliefs about your Self. That's the only change required.

———————

"I finally admitted that what I believed wasn't working. Then I could try something I didn't believe. It worked."

SONDRA ANICE BARNES

———————

This day is the only day of this particular date you'll ever have for this lifetime. Whatever you do today is your gift to life. What gifts are you choosing to share?

———————

Harried is one way to spend time. Rarely productive, long-term. But it does serve a purpose. What would you face if you gave it up? It's surely a stressor.

———————

Do you fill your life with deadlines to the exclusion of love-lines? If so, you serve Self-punishment, not Self-fulfillment.

———————

When we are out of touch with our feelings, we disconnect and deny. Then we unplug our humanness.

———⎯∽⎯———

Not till I make peace with what is, not till I name reality, am I positioned for solution.

———⎯∽⎯———

Find a person with no problems and you'll find a corpse.

———⎯∽⎯———

Thoughts birth feelings. Feelings birth behaviors. How you treat others mirrors how you think-feel about your Self. (Remember that when someone misbehaves with you.) You can decide to think anew. What you think, you create. Remember, behavior matches the self-image.

———⎯∽⎯———

Self-pity is like a wet diaper. At first it makes you feel warm and comfy. Then it begins to sting . . . Self and Others.

Gentle self-compassion, however, is not to be confused with self-pity.

———⎯∽⎯———

"While being protective of young children is appropriate, protecting adults is Self-protection once removed."

JANIS OLSEN

———⎯∽⎯———

When you overreact, the present has triggered a past tender place. You can use that internal flag to rework the original pain, to stand free of invisible loads—past beliefs.

Resist releasing past stuff? Cling to old patterns? Ignore old decisions that no longer fit? If so, you get to rehash . . . over and over and over.

———◦⟨∞⟩◦———

Probably none of us likes the idea that we create much of our own world. We'd rather think it was others. Who else, however, creates the fear? Limit? Unmet expectation? Choice? Attitude?

Unconsciously, like it or not, we create our inner experience and decide how to handle it. Once we accept this, however, we realize we have the power to rewrite the script, redirect the play, recast the characters.

There are few adult victims, only volunteers.

———◦⟨∞⟩◦———

Consistently passive people wait for "it" to come to them. For others to provide. Sidelined.

Consistently active people make "it" happen. They take hold. Mainstream.

Guess which group is happier according to studies.

Life asks us to be involved. Anything less is simply less life.

———◦⟨∞⟩◦———

Develop your talents so that you know you have something to offer. Then you're not a spectator in life. Who cares if your gift is less than perfect? Or if others have more? Giving your gift joins you to life. You were not born to incubate.

Sidelines are not lifelines.

Listening to Body Talk

Physical symptoms are barometers saying, "Do something different." Change attitude, belief, lifestyle or how you relate. Avoid changing and your body will make the next message louder, stronger.

Symptoms have payoff. Search for how to get the same payoff without the symptom. Or maybe you need to erase the need for that particular payoff.

"I've got to keep proving myself," for instance, is a killer. Why not lay aside that self-pitchfork?

———✧———

Your body has the final word. If you ask it to deliver beyond its limits, it cooperates for a while. Then it goes on strike. Illness is the body's personal message. Nature will not be violated for long.

———✧———

"Complete health and awakening are really the same."

TARTHANG TULKU

———✧———

If you believe we create illness by negative beliefs, then you know we create wellness by positive beliefs.

———✧———

The most malignant cancer is self-hate. It lies at the root of all destructive behavior. And symptomatology.

———•∞•———

Will you seek afar to quell the inner unrest? Out there, in many places, in others?

Eventually you will come back to things best known to you, finding happiness, knowledge, not in another place, but in the inner space. Not for another hour, but for this hour.

———•∞•———

Seek, strive, go for it against all odds. *Make* it happen.

Let it go, let it go, release. *Let* it happen.

Confusing? Both are true. Listen to your body's wisdom. It knows when and where.

Imperfect Is Perfect

If we try to be perfect, to always be right, we set ourselves up to lose. We are not God.

It is important to live this.

———•∞•———

"Perfect" only pushes others away. Yet we go for "perfect" so others won't reject. The *perfect* double bind. Claiming fallibility means embracing imperfection . . . our admission ticket to the human race.

———•∞•———

Perfectionism is the perfect way to be enslaved to the tyranny of discontent.

———•∞•———

A main source of unhappiness lies in expectations too high. Perfection's demand wants all *or* none. It rejects dark *and* light. It makes "little" "Big." When you accept reality, you rejoice that imperfect is perfect.

———————

Go for progress, not completion, if your project is your own growth. You are never really "finished."

———————

To continue to search "out there" is to prolong making a commitment to "in here." It is to prolong deciding to wake.

———————

You are enough. Be it. Throw out any input that says otherwise. Just "get" that you *are* enough, warts and all. And before you know it, the warts will disappear or become assets. Because once you "get" it, you will only be able to walk in Light. And act accordingly.

———————

Obsession is not necessarily negative. Become obsessed with the positive. Focus on hope, wonder, gentle, new. Pour energy into meditation and self-honesty. Become obsessed with the power of Love. Obsess on letting go that which needs releasing.

This positive attitude and outgoing action fuel your Heartsong into reality.

———————

When you really affirm yourself, you spend your energy doing your purpose . . . playing your Heartsong . . . because it feels good. Invariably, it gives good to all others. If not, it is not Heartsong.

———————

Go where there is no trail. And leave a path of clarity for others to follow.

Emerging is an emergency.
How do I, how do you, answer the call? We answer daily.

Do you feel you have no Heartsong because you are less talented, less educated, have produced no tangible work?

Your Ph.D. may be in outreach, in the warmth of your smile, in your tender empathy when another falters. It may be in your ongoing courage no matter what. Intangibles that tangibly affect: warmth, tenacity, risking, forgiveness, honesty, truth, decency, faith.

Your word of encouragement may make more impact on the fabric of one human life than the grandest monument ever built.

Heartsongs come multiply packaged. Avoid discounting yours.

Sartre said, "To choose is a choice. Not to choose is a choice. You cannot not choose."

Most of us are *unaware* that we constantly make choices that are either for or against wholeness. Partnered with Source, your choices cannot be other than pure. Unpartnered, you miss your Heartsong.

Your gift came with you. It will die with you if you refuse to awaken it. To avoid your Heartsong is to

choose to withhold from the human race. You can
choose to enrich humanity by outpouring your Song
. . . giving your gift in Love.

Remember, you cannot not choose.

SOURCE

I nner peace. Who would refuse it? We seek it in countless
ways . . . accumulating, pleasuring, busying, goaling.
These can bring satisfactions along the way. But too often
such does not last. Getting does not give permanent peace.

Ongoing serenity, the kind that sticks through thick and
thin, is most likely when we meet life with confidence and
purpose. Then we come from an inner groundedness. Then
we know who we truly are. And we have a sense of purpose
and meaning.

Does inner peace free us from problems and conflict? Not
at all. But inner harmony lets us cope with what comes very
differently than otherwise. Operating from inner directed-
ness means we are simply less buffeted. This center gives
calm to handle storm.

You may not find that this section speaks to you if you are
a doubter. I invite you to merely think of nature. We can
hardly deny that a Life Force pulsates through it. We know
the rhythm of the seasons. We see life, unfolding, loss,
change, death, rebirth over and over everywhere. We see balance and equilibrium in nature. And an impeccable order
micro- and macrocosmically. We know that when there is
lack of balance . . . lack of harmony . . . a price is paid.

Like it or not, we are inextricably linked to this universal order. We are in a dance with the universal song.

Fear, doubt, worry, mistrust, jealousy, greed throw us out of balance. Their antithesis—love that is single-minded, predictably positive—puts us back into harmony. In Love we are positive energy channels. Our lives make a constructive difference.

You know you are unique. Of course. But let's see *how unique.*

The DNA molecule determines your inherited qualities. Mathematicians estimate that the DNA molecule can theoretically unite in $10^{2,400,000,000}$ ways. By comparison they estimate that the entire universe contains only 10^{76} atomic particles.* This means that to find two people genetically strung together alike you'd need $10^{2,400,000,000}$ people.

Mind-boggling!

To grasp the enormity of this number, realize what you would need simply to write out this figure. If each zero were one inch wide, you would need a strip of paper 37,000 miles long!

If you translated this figure into units its enormity becomes even more staggering. Robert Jastrow, one of our leading astronomers, estimates the size of our universe as ten billion light-years.† There are six trillion miles in one light-year. If you took dots one millimeter in diameter and laid them end to end *from our earth to the end of our universe and back* you would have to do that $10^{399,999,977}$ times to equal $10^{2,400,000,000}$!‡

Now do you realize how rare you are?

The likelihood of another genetically put together into your unique pattern at any time in the past, anywhere today or any time in the future is so infinitesimally small as to be inconceivable. And this uniqueness is quite apart from all the conditioning that has been reacted to by this uniqueness of yours.

To say that you are a special event in the universe is not Pollyanna drivel. It is a fact of life.

How irrelevant to compare yourself to another! How totally impossible to try to be a carbon copy! Our universe does not indulge in duplicates. Each creation is virtually unrepeatable.

Do you know who You truly are?

You are an unprecedented event in the universe!

You are not a world premiere; you are a universal one!

You are an expression of the Source.

No person, thing or event can erase this truth.

Stop and concretely experience the magnitude of this fact. Let it sink deep into your bones and tissues. Feel its impact.

This awareness doesn't mean you look at others with disdain, for you realize they too are as rare as You. A lasting and responsible value system falls more easily into place when you are in touch with the wonder of You and the wonder of others. If I see the negatives in you, I see the outer, the behavior, the appearance. I see what separates us.

If I see the True You, I see the Inner. I see what unites us.

Do you want to see a miracle? All you have to do is look in the mirror! All you have to do is look around you! Each of us is made of the same Life Stuff. Yet each of us is in essence without peer. . . .

The Real You represents a separate entity in the vastness of Creation. *New but related beyond time and space to all others . . . to all Creation.*

This Source is called God. Awesome in creativity . . . awesome in omnipotence . . . awesome in omnipresence. We come from this Source, move in It, have our being in It. There is not a spot where God is not.

This section is to remind that we are a trinity: body, mind and spirit. Let any one go off balance and inner peace goes askew.

Those with ongoing serenity do not neglect spirit. Indeed, they know that spirit is Source. For when we *experientially* center in Love, body and mind heal to become whole. The peace that surpasseth understanding is about that wholeness. We are at one. And it is then that we most clearly find and sing our Heartsong.

The song "Let There Be Peace on Earth and Let It Begin with Me" says it all. This planet cannot fully heal until we each individually come to Peace.

And that means coming to Love. To Source. To God.

You have heard it said, "Life is God's gift to you; what you do with your life is your gift to God."
What *are* you doing with that gift?

———⋘———

"What lies behind us and what lies before us are small matters compared to what lies within us."

RALPH WALDO EMERSON

———⋘———

To have loneliness, we do what creates it. Fear of hurt, outreach, risk spring from Source separation. We cannot escape God. We can only turn our backs on Him. Once connected, we fear not fear. Unified with Love, fear falls away.

———⋘———

When we stop resisting that we are alone, we discover we are not. We can *believe* we are alone but that doesn't make it so. No one can do our birthing, joying, paining, dying for us. To know that we are one with life —that we are from and of Source—changes aloneness to all-one-ness.

Our whole world changes with this simple reposition.

———⋘———

When water is swift, when storms rage inside, ask, "Who is in charge? God or me?" The answer calms the churn.

———⋘———

There is no such thing as a quick fix in life. Growth takes time . . . a lifetime.

Pain and loss quilt with joy and finding. Life is process. Yet, rooted in God, you stand firm, knowing that dark patterns Light.

———⌒———

Saying "no" to fear is saying "yes" to hope. When fear is greater than hope, we use energy for despair and destruction. When hope is greater than fear, we use it for wholeness and healing.

Fear and hope are two sides of your *belief*.

- That which I feared came upon me.
- My words shall prosper in the thing in which I send them.
- Whatsoever things you ask in prayer, *believing* you shall receive.
- It is done unto you *as* you believe.

Where are you placing your belief energy?

———⌒———

"Even God cannot change the past."
                                                    AGATHON

———⌒———

Every day, in every happening—loss or gain—life gives us a chance to reflect God.

———⌒———

We are each given the daily choice to affirm and love or to withdraw and blame.

It is human to vote the latter. It is a gift to God when we vote love.

Filling inner void with things from the outside never works for long. Filling it with Source Food does.

To center in Source, to know you have Purpose lets you shed low and shaky self-esteem—the cause of destructive living. Then you fly free.

A negative self-image is like a barnacle. It needs shedding. Go within to the Unconditioned Self . . . the Real You. There will all be made known.

Only I limit me. No "yes, but's"! I avoid limitation when I *know* who I truly am. God travels with us everywhere, in us, as us. And God is without limitation.

If we put our True Self down, we put down God's creation. Ever wonder how He feels about this discount?

We continue to make God inadequate when we place our human limits on Him. We stop making God inadequate when we refuse limitation and lack. We walk as the miracle of the Hologram.

Enlightenment is not being blissed out, withdrawn or lethargic. To drop out is to lose our sense of responsibility for Self and to Others. True centeredness carries with it a thrust for life, a push to fulfill our purpose. We are here to connect and be connected.

Even so, before enlightenment you will do laundry; after enlightenment you will do laundry.

———⚬———

Enlightenment—standing in the Light—is not without ebb and flow. Its coming and going are part of the process. The final arriving comes after.

———⚬———

We are made in the image and likeness of God. When we betray His trust, we let God down.

———⚬———

All true Power lies only in Spirit. Only the energy of Love in the long run allows us to overcome.

———⚬———

Since faith moves mountains, why not be a mountain mover in your life?

———⚬———

Every father who truly loves sets standards for his children. He requires they be accountable. He asks not for empty words but for responsible behavior.

Even so God the Father. He asks that we live right over wrong. He does not deal in sloppy *agape*.

———⚬———

God doesn't like taking dictation. He never applied for the job of secretary. When meditating, see and affirm the highest good for all concerned; be nonattached to outcome; release to "Thy will be done." There is a Grander Plan.

———◦∽◦———

Healing comes when we get our egos (Conditioned Self) out of the way and let Love in.

———◦∽◦———

None of us is an accident in God's eyes. Even if others told you so, remember they are not God. Each of us is born with a Heartsong . . . a special gift God wants brought into the world. It carries our own fingerprint . . . like no other. Remember, we are here to learn lessons, develop our talents, give them to the world, to love and then return Home. Our assignment is to leave the world a little better because we walked through.

More often than not, we find that purpose, we claim, refine, hone it out of the fire of pain, grief, loss, devastation. Knowing this empowers us to overcome . . . to connect . . . to accomplish our mission. It allows us to celebrate Life no matter what the loss.

As we each transform, at some level, we elevate all human life.

———◦∽◦———

"Be still and know." If we do not choose still times, we starve spiritually. We need connection not just with head but with heart, mind, body . . . at a cellular level. When we do, we claim sonship and daughtership. Daily pressures stay but reactions change. Barriers and abrasives become ripples. Unshakable comes from unbroken connection.

———◦∽◦———

"Enough of this prayer stuff, I want God with skin on!" We have exactly that. He comes every day with skin on. He comes with every person whose life we touch. We can choose to see Him everywhere if we will but awake. He speaks if we listen. But God is nonverbal.

So many look for "right" relationship. Decoded, this means one that makes us safe, unlonely, cared for; one that affirms in spite of our warts. We search for the Grand Parent.

Why not go for the ultimate safety? The ultimate *Grand Parent?*

Groundedness in Source is the only right relationship. Then we Self-nurture. We move to manifest our song. Then all relationships are right because we do not ask others to fill our empty spaces. We connect from joy and invulnerability. We outflow from overflow.

The only power worth having, the only power corruption-free, is the Higher Power.

Love boomerangs only when it has no strings.

Can you see things as on loan to you? Youth, possessions, status, relationships, your body? They may or may not be around a while. The truth is . . . you never own them. Advantageous as they may be, they do not bring peace per se. How attached, how intensely you "need," equals the pain of their loss.

What is not on loan is: your awareness and faith; your belief in Love's Principle; your refusal to give up; your acceptance of reality; your conviction that Light dispels Dark; your determination to live Love; your trust in God. These you can truly possess. To root in these universals gives lasting anchorage.

"People have points *of* view . . . God has points *to* view."

If you are a reactor, you are forever tied to situation. If it is to your liking, you're happy. If not, you're sad. Grounded in Source, you are free from situation. Such connectedness gives invulnerability.

As children, naively we borrow Others' views and see ourselves accordingly. And constantly compare. Growing up means waking up—to who we truly are. We do not take *that* journey until we give up dependency on others and situations. That dependency is a choice for quicksand.

Let no person, no event define or diminish your Real Self. You are here for good . . . for God.

The "I" of You is apart from name, age, body, status, sex, role. The "I" of You is your Real Self . . . Soul . . . Spirit. You are a nonmaterial essence dwelling in your particular package.

We diminish ourselves when we refuse to acknowledge who we truly are. When we do not celebrate the wonder of our firstness and that of others, we fail to fulfill the Promise.

———⌒———

Slip into faith. Know that Love *is* a real force.

———⌒———

Crucifying self-centered getting and power trips may be a daily process. But as nonmaterial beings, we are asked to live Love. How we vote is reflected in how we live. In what we value and commit to.

———⌒———

Many believe that rituals, buildings, words and certain studies make them spiritual. They are assists. It is *what* is in our hearts; it is *how* we walk with others that affirms our connection to God. We cannot hurt those who trust us; we cannot misbehave with family, friends, business and know God. We either *live* Love daily or we separate from God.

Being human, we will be tempted and fall short. But we correct as soon as we can. Integrity, fair play and decency are rooted in God. We either live Love or we do not. Daily we choose what we honor. If it cannot be held up to the Light, it is not of God.

———⌒———

The universe, as you know, is not into carbon copies. Uniqueness is a constant; a given. Comparisons are an insult. Our job is to know that uniqueness, which is paradoxically non-unique in that it is a droplet of the Whole.

Universal Order says grow, change, come into newness. Keep your channel clean. Make your "firstness" shine.

———— ⸎ ————

"God, grant me the serenity to accept the things I cannot change, the courage to change the things I can and the wisdom to know the difference." St. Augustine's prayer is a statement that human power has limits.

God power does not.

———— ⸎ ————

We transcend when we know that we are not the Point.

DR. SANDRA SEAGAL (paraphrased)

———— ⸎ ————

"Except ye become as a little child . . ." The little child sees with the eyes of innocence. Afresh, without judgment, without expectations, without hardening of the categories.

———— ⸎ ————

We most fear death when we have not lived life moment by moment and enjoyed.

———— ⸎ ————

In polarities there is unity.

———— ⸎ ————

You *are* the gift. You are the treasure. You are already "there." Accept this is so.

———— ⸎ ————

Know these truths about you. Chant them within: "I am a child of the Creative Source. I am worth abundance, peace and health. I am rich from an Infinite Source of Love."

———— ∞ ————

Why do you search for love?
You *are* Love.

———— ∞ ————

The deepest Self within is the God Self.
Take the Question there.
Listen in silence.

———— ∞ ————

Atonement is At-one-ment with Self, World, God.
We are all being invited to At-one-ment.

———— ∞ ————

"As the battle rages 'round me . . .
    I am glad to have found that I am *not* the General.
    And that His Love for me
    Is the source of everything I need.
    With Him as the General,
    I need only learn to salute and march.
    The Celebration can then begin—
        Where the salute becomes the embrace,
        And the march becomes the dance."
                                        MICHAEL J. KENDALL

———— ∞ ————

We are meant to be Lamplighters through love and service. But we turn on the glow of another's lamp only

if our own flame burns clear and bright. Remember,
that's why we're here . . . to Lamplight.

It is the Father within that doeth the work.
How can He do the work if we refuse to go within
and meet?
    Or refuse to cooperate?
    Or release?
    Or forgive?

Faith in the Overall means knowing some outcomes
are beyond our understanding. With faith we trust that
we can overcome even so. Because a benign Force in the
Universe supports us. God.

We awaken, we transform, when we know we are a
channel. Awakening comes with

   • a change in attitude toward Self and Other;
   • a knowing that we never walk alone;
   • an experiential relationship to God;
   • a commitment to living Truth.

All else is peripheral. Each of us is being asked to *awake*
. . . now. Serenity requires we hear . . . and respond.

Wedding Light to Love
And taking that Power out to the world
Is the Mission.

With God all things are possible.

NOTES

RELATIONSHIPS

11 The two subselves that cause havoc and prevent joy are the
Critic and Not-OK selves. The former dishes out the pain;
the latter feeds on that pain. For specifics on how to remove
the energy from these tapes, refer to Dorothy Corkille
Briggs, *Celebrate Your Self* (Garden City, N.Y.: Doubleday &
Company, 1977).

36–37 Paul Brenner, M.D., *Health Is a Question of Balance* (New York:
Vantage Press, 1978).

41 Catherine Ponder, *The Dynamic Laws of Healing* (Marina del
Rey, Calif.: Devorss & Co., 1966).

LOSS

72–73 Paul S. McElroy, *Words of Comfort* (Mount Vernon, N.Y.: Peter
Pauper Press, 1968).

LIFE

101 Sondra Anice Barnes, *Life Is the Way It Is* (Reseda, Calif.:
Brason-Sarger Publications, P.O. Box 842, 1978).

112 Reprint from Dorothy Corkille Briggs, *Celebrate Your Self*
(Garden City, N.Y.: Doubleday & Company, 1977).

112   * David Beramini and Editors of *Life, Mathematics* (New York: Time, Inc., 1963).

112   † Robert Jastrow, *Red Giants and White Dwarfs.* (New York: Harper & Row, 1967).

112   ‡ I am indebted to Dr. Robert A. Smith, Professor of Statistics and Computer Design, Chairman of Department of Educational Psychology, University of Southern California, for this calculation.

121   Fynn, *Mister God, This Is Anna* (New York: Holt, Rinehart & Winston, 1974).